Thrifty

LIVING THE FRUGAL LIFE WITH STYLE

WITHDRAWN FROM EVLD

MARJORIE HARRIS

ANANSI

This edition published in 2010 by
House of Anansi Press Inc.
110 Spadina Avenue, Suite 801
Toronto, ON, M5V 2K4
Tel. 416-363-4343
Fax 416-363-1017
www.anansi.ca

Distributed in Canada by
HarperCollins Canada Ltd.
1995 Markham Road
Scarborough, ON, M1B 5M8
Toll free tel. 1-800-387-0117

Distributed in the United States by
Publishers Group West
1700 Fourth Street
Berkeley, CA 94710
Toll free tel. 1-800-788-3123

House of Anansi Press is committed to protecting our natural environment.
As part of our efforts, this book is printed on paper that contains
100% post-consumer recycled fibres, is acid-free, and is processed chlorine-free.

14   13   12   11   10   2   3   4   5   6

LIBRARY AND ARCHIVES CANADA CATALOGING IN PUBLICATION

Harris, Marjorie
Thrifty : living the frugal life with style / Marjorie Harris.

ISBN 978-0-88784-832-2

1. Thriftiness. 2. Consumer education. 3. Finance, Personal.
I. Title.

TX335 H37 2009   640.73   C2009-903906-0

Library of Congress Control Number: 2009929648

Text design and typesetting: Sari Naworynski

We acknowledge for their financial support of our publishing program
the Canada Council for the Arts, the Ontario Arts Council, and the Government of Canada
through the Canada Book Fund.

Printed and bound in Canada

For Jack

CONTENTS

HOW I GOT TO BE
THRIFTY

The day always begins with this Zen moment: it's time to line up the numbers, check the bank accounts, to add and subtract. I know where the money is and where it's going. Thus I know where I'm going. I was trained to respect and use money very carefully.

Money is partly the subject of this book. But it's more about what smart people do with it: how they use it wisely and make very little go a long way. It's about finding pleasure in small economies and the large ideas that can come to fruition with attention to details.

Literary legend Margaret Atwood, who recently wrote the wonderful *Payback: Debt and the Shadow Side of Wealth*, suggested her publishers explore the other side of the coin — a practical companion piece, so to speak, on how to apply thrift and frugality to our daily lives — and that I should write it. "You have to interview me," she said.

When we were having tea one day discussing ideas about thrift, Margaret brought out a big old ledger from the 1930s. It was her mother's carefully kept daily record of every penny she spent, on what and to whom. This extraordinary document is a social history of the Atwood family, and reinforced my own feeling that knowing exactly where you are at any moment financially is a healthy way to be.

Margaret Atwood has always been a thrifty person; she came from a practical home: "My father put himself through university living in a tent, and he sent money home to his family." Her mother also lived in extreme circumstances; she raised two of her three kids in the bush. So thrift was second nature to her own family as well.

"Keeping a frugal house is about keeping your home in running order," Margaret says, "without having to pay other people to do it and without spending a lot of money. It's about doing things yourself."

Margaret and I have this much of a shared background: she had a mother distracted by a sick child, and I had a mother with a terminal disease. I gradually started doing most of the cooking, though not all of the cleaning, at age ten. By twelve, the transition for responsibility of the house had slipped from mother to daughter.

"It was a factor in our youth," Margaret says. "We all had chores. There was an expectation that, as a twelve-year-old, you were perfectly capable of taking over the household duties. My parents had done so, and they thought that's just how people were. By nine, you knew how to clean the toilet, polish the silver, dust. Kids just did those tasks."

She points out that we were also taught how to do a ton of other things that are now considered demeaning or sexist to teach children (unless they go to Scouts or Guides): how to sew a button; proper ironing techniques; how to hem almost any garment; replacing elastics; basic cooking methods; how to shine shoes. Our mothers may have handed these tasks on to us, but they were also a part of the core curriculum at school. Home Economics, alas, was confined to girls, while boys went to Shop and learned how to use a saw and run a lathe. We were taught these things to help us survive and to be frugal people. These courses are no longer on any curriculum, and now these skills have to be reinvented and relearned.

Money became a guiding light in my life the minute I found out I could earn it. But money also plagued our house: there just never seemed to be enough. And though my parents were frugal, and always had paying hobbies, they did need a little bit of help. I was so good with money as a child they'd occasionally borrow from me for their own needs: a car, for instance. I knew I had paid for at least the front right wheel of our Oldsmobile. That they didn't think it was important to pay me back hurt. But it did make me wary of ever lending money to anybody, especially family and friends. I learned early on that money can interfere with relationships.

As good Baptists, we were also trained to tithe (10 percent came off the top of every penny earned to be put toward charity); we learned that if you were a fine person and became clever with money, good things would come your way. Thus money and parents, money and the church, money and the pleasant things of life, money and work were all bound together in one large complicated package. It took a broken marriage or two to find out that the spending of it could also waylay depression or become an expensive way to avoid reality.

I've never earned a lot of money in my life. I make enough most of the time, but I've had periods in which there was no money. When I say there was no money, it's not the euphemism a lot of my wealthier friends use when they mean they are down to their last few millions or hundreds of thousands (it's hard to make the distinction when you haven't got it). When we had no money, there was no money at all.

With my father being a padre in the RCAF, and my mother a proper senior officer's wife, we abided by the rules of the Officers' Mess at the dinner table: no conversation about sex, religion, or politics. Among the delicious subjects left was money. It was pretty good training for a future as a journalist. I always want to know how much things cost, how much people make, and just how they live on their incomes.

Because my father was a minister, he was also privy to what was going on in everyone's lives (at least the Protestants'). And since we were to be seen and not heard, we little pitchers had big ears. The talk of money is everywhere when there isn't much around. So it was a shock when I ventured into the wider world to find that people were appalled by any open discussion about money. Having it was dirty, getting it was nasty, and not having any at all was a character flaw.

My first exposure to thrift happened on September 15 when I turned six. I was deemed old enough to receive an allowance in exchange for completing chores around the house (heretofore done for free). I took the 25 cents, went alone to the local candy store, and spent the whole lot. I managed to eat everything: candy bars, red and black licorice, a few chewy pipes, and a lot of hard candy.

When I got home, I threw up in the walkway beside our house. My mother said (yelled perhaps): "You spent it all? Are you crazy?" From that day forward I spent very little money on candy. I decided if I wanted candy, I would complete extra chores and save my allowance. I generally made myself useful to anyone, not just family, if there was a quarter attached to it: wash dishes, polish floors, as well as the usual babysitting. I gathered blueberries and raspberries, selling them for 25 cents a quart, which led to a decades-long loathing of these fruits.

After my very first experience with the big splurge, I knew money could make you sick both physically and psychically. I also intuited that if you had it you had to save it: there would be hard times ahead.

The money struggles meant that my mother and father always had discreet paying hobbies to make a little extra. My father did (and I use that word correctly) photography. He wasn't terribly good at it, but he could compose pictures better than most. For years the bathtub was filled with negatives. And one little room was always used for developing photographs.

My mother did everything from decorating picture frames with seashells, to hand-tinting Dad's pictures, to selling Beauty Counsellor products from the house (they didn't sell well, and we had enough stuff to smear on our faces for years).

She worked and worked. She made all of our clothes. During the war when Dad was overseas, he sent her some fabric, which she immediately turned into a suit for my brother and dresses for my baby sister and I, along with a jacket for herself. It was the first time she'd seen a bolt of material for years — rich blue velvet. Then came the letter of explanation: the fabric was for an altar cloth.

Their worst side job was inspired by *The Egg and I*, a memoir about a young wife who moves with her husband to the countryside to run a poultry farm. They invested all of our money, including mine, in chickens. Between the chickens in the backyard, the fermenting fig wine in the dining room (they did like the odd tipple), and the smell of blood and feathers emanating from the basement during hunting season, we seemed to be foraging all the time. These experiences certainly set me up for a life as a freelance writer, never knowing when a cheque might come in.

My father was killed in a plane crash when I was seventeen years old. We found that he had left a no-flying clause in his insurance, so we were bereft in more ways than one. He was a grieving widower (my mother had died eighteen months before), and he hadn't read his insurance policy properly. This experience taught me to always read contracts (usually) very carefully. But nothing prepared us for the way we were treated as orphans. The air force gave him a bang-up funeral, handed me the two weeks' pay he was owed, and said, "No widow, no pension."

Our guardian/uncle worked furiously to get any compensation for us kids. The government, eventually and very reluctantly, forked over a monthly stipend if we went on to post-secondary education. So with only a couple of jobs I could get through university without owing a bucket of money.

While in graduate school, I got married and learned the hard way that if you cannot discuss money before the wedding, you sure won't be able to after. When I presented my then-husband with a budget, I thought he'd walk out on the spot. Neither of us realized what little money we had, how many bills had to be paid, and what having a baby was going to do to this volatile situation. I offered to be the family accountant, which meant he had to give me his salary and live on an allowance. It didn't work. And neither did the marriage. I learned you should always agree to discuss (or get help with) money before you tie the knot. You should consider signing a pre-nuptial agreement, even if it is just to organize a budget.

So in my early twenties I became a single mother with an alcoholic non-support-paying ex-husband. I realized I was going to have to pay my own way and learned never to count on anyone else for survival, for me or my two kids. When I went into a second marriage, we agreed we'd control our own incomes, sort out who would pay what bills and on time. I'd found Mr. Reliable — to my enormous relief.

Then I got a credit card on the advice of my accountant. "It will keep everything in one place," he explained. "You'll see how much you are spending and on what." One card meant a new and vast world of credit opened up to me: not only did I sign up for a Visa and MasterCard, but department store cards such as Holt Renfrew, Creed's, The Bay, and Eaton's. Neither my accountant nor I knew I'd end up using credit in a wild and emotional way when my world fell apart, as it did in spades when my second marriage failed. I was broke and miserable — so I shopped. I attempted to pay the minimum interest on all of them, but I didn't stop shopping. When my accountant confiscated my cards, he took away my best friends, my booze, my addiction.

I bought gorgeous stuff and gave most of it away but kept one pair of insanely high-heeled Bruno Magli boots. Though I can't possibly wear them anymore, they are a reminder of what can happen when you use credit for emotional support: danger, waste, and dark days ahead.

It took a couple of years and a *huge* amount of discipline to retrieve my old frugal ways. I ditched all the cards but one, and never charged another thing until it was completely paid off. I still pay off the monthly balance, and I never shop for stuff I can't afford, which is the essence of the thrifty life.

Long since reconciled with my second husband, Jack Batten, we've kept this old house going and have had a wonderful life. There were a few milestones along the way. I was a dedicated smoker. And when I decided to quit I did it cold turkey, promising myself that every penny I'd have spent on a package of cigarettes would go into a travel fund. After one year, we had enough money to afford a European holiday. It astounded me how easy it was to save: money was fun.

Still, I've realized that no matter how careful you are, sometimes events blindside you. I spent twelve glorious years at *Gardening Life* magazine. It was the world's most perfect job: writing about gardening and getting paid a regular fee for my presence on the magazine. After years and years of hardscrabble freelance writing, this was the ultimate luxury — regular money.

There was never a medical, dental, or pension plan, no vacation pay and no expense account. But it was still the best deal I'd ever had. However, I got lulled into a sense of security, something no free-lancer (writer, actor, artist, entrepreneur) should ever do. I was not prepared for the shock when the magazine abruptly folded and I was out of a job.

Though I had socked some money away in an emergency account, when I got laid off I was definitely not prepared emotionally. It was scary beyond belief. But this book has come about and once again money is guiding my life in its own weird way.

We talked to dozens and dozens of inspiring people who were willing to talk about money and how they use it well. (My son Chris Harris devised the questionnaires and did a huge amount of research.) We stuck with the people we know who live the frugal life with style, and the word went out like the old pebble in the pond, rippling widely.

Money can be depressing or exhilarating. The contributors to this book have decided to make it fun, thrilling, an adventure. And that's what we're trying to do in this book: to look at how we save, how we spend, and how to do it with style.

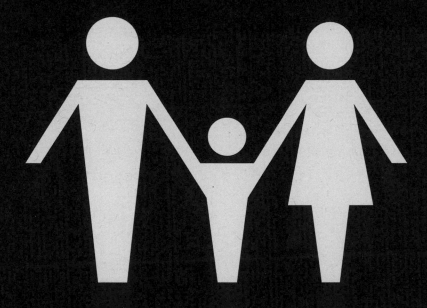

CHAPTER 1

THE THRIFTY CITIZEN

You don't wake up one morning and say, "Well, now, I think I'll become thrifty." It sneaks up on you, or perhaps you get trained to mind your money from a young age. Or maybe you are simply born with a frugal gene. I got trained into leading a thrifty life; what was a family habit of frugality became a personal one. It was the beginning of a lifelong game: how much can I save in spite of the odds? I still have bank books kept from when I was a youth. I love looking at them. Do I remember every cent I've ever spent? Of course not. But looking at those books pulls the strings of memories together in a most intricate way — I marvel at how I managed in those days.

This chapter looks at thrifty citizens. And if there's anything they share it's that they're in control of their finances and their associated desires. They are neither controlled by money nor the temptations of the material world around us. They understand the need to save on small things in order to attain the big things in life — without remorse. These people also share the feeling that they love everything they do, from shopping for food, to how they dress, to taking care of their homes. They thrive, and this sense of thriftiness has a long history.

In the thirteenth century to be thrifty meant you were doing well. By the nineteenth century the meaning had shifted to suggest good economic management. But at the turn of the twentieth century, thrifty had come to be associated with frugality — of living a sparse, economical life. Both thrift and frugality had taken on the tarnish of stinginess or meanness (think Ebenezer Scrooge). Now, once again, we are looking at thrifty with another view: today it suggests that one is thriving, while at the same time being mindful of where every penny goes, from buying food to a new car.

So thrifty citizens never went away, just underground. Now they are emerging once again, showing us how they manage money, how they save by being smart shoppers, and how they savour the good stuff of life. This is the life we want to lead: the life that saves to live, but does it with a delicious sense of style.

THRIFTY VS CHEAP, WANTS VS NEED

Our relationship with money — and by association with the material world — is not just about necessity, nor is it all about deep desires or wants. It's about finding a balance between needs and wants, and being satisfied with that balance. There is no fun to be had always feeling slightly dissatisfied; it's as bad as constantly feeling hungry. So uncovering what you must have, and figuring out what you can do without, is the first step toward becoming a thrifty citizen.

Margaret Atwood, very definitely a thrifty citizen, says, "Materialism is mistaking quantity with quality. The point is not having stuff, the point is appreciating the stuff you have. Adding to the pile is not going to make you feel any better. Money is a symbol. The acquisitors are in it for the *grrrrr* factor. 'I, alpha chimp, am bigger than other alpha chimps.' They don't actually need any more things — they need more bragging and chest-thumping rights."

As Atwood points out, what we lost in our rush to acquire more material goods and status symbols was how to value what we already have. The push to be bigger and better was part of the whole ethos of what describes success, and we lost our handle on just how much is enough.

"There are two uses of the word 'more,'" Atwood says. "There's Oliver Twist saying 'I need more because I'm starving.' Then there's the Edward G. Robinson character in the film *Key Largo*. Humphrey Bogart says to him, 'What do you want?' and Edward G. Robinson replies, 'I dunno. I dunno what I want.' Bogart says, 'I'll tell you what you want: you want more.' Robinson says, 'That's right, I want more of everything. I want more.' And that 'more' is the more of greed.

"More from greed is about power, not need. After all, how many steaks can you eat in one day? Not many. The rest is symbolic. Being good with money means that you always have some, you're always just a tiny bit ahead of the game. It's not *have more*, it's *do more*. It really is about how to do more with less, and it means you are in control of your life."

In this new age, being branded a shopaholic means you haven't sorted out the difference between your needs (not that much) and your wants (more). Defining the difference between the two is the first step toward living a more frugal life and becoming a thrifty citizen.

Thrift is so muddled with the idea of cheapness that it's a source of great irritation to frugal types. Cheap is someone who buys based only on price, whose life experiences are guided by price, and who would probably give up something sublime because it costs too much. The rules of thrift aren't meant to develop a stingy quality; indeed, it should bring on a feeling of well-being rather deprivation. To thrive is all-important. Being thrifty requires a brain; being cheap doesn't. Being thrifty is figuring out how things work and making them work more efficiently. Being thrifty means being self-aware.

It's having this full life that interests me as it spins around money. So often the getting of money, amassing of the same, the building of profits obscures everything else, including the ability to see the extraordinary wonder of the world and how we fit into a small part of it. A garden isn't just a garden. It's also an ecological system where every-thing relates to everything else, every aspect of it is interdependent. Destroy just one aspect of this great body or form and you harm it in some way. Money is also an ecological system. When you concentrate on only one aspect of it — the getting of it, the spending of it, the *grrrrr* factor, as Atwood puts it — you mess up some part of the healthy whole. The enjoyment of making your money do as much as possible is getting back to those basics.

Understanding the difference between wants and needs means understanding that some things *are* worth more than others. For many, this concept is difficult to grasp and does not necessarily come with maturity. It means knowing yourself and your life very well, elements of which are changing all the time. We talked to young people who understood clearly the difference between their wants and needs. They had instinctively divined this healthy balance at an early age. Observation? Probably. They likely had good role models in their parents. What was shocking was the number of older people who just didn't get it, who thought of frugality as some moral, austere value, who equated thrift with cheapness.

The distinction between wants and needs is critical for how satisfied you feel as a frugal person, especially one with style. When push comes to shove, my needs are as follows: delicious organic food, decent wine and candles, and my beloved to talk to. I would hate doing without these modest luxuries, this person. Wherever they are, I can make a home. Without them, I am bereft. But when I go out and buy these items, no matter what financial state we are in, I feel rich. Everyone has a list like this one. If you don't, then start jotting down your needs. You'll be amazed at what you learn about yourself: the values that embody your way of life and being. It's the first step toward self-awareness and the thrifty way of life.

LEARNING THE THRIFTY WAY OF LIFE
By Former Governor General Adrienne Clarkson

Anyone who has fled their homeland across five oceans with their family and one suitcase apiece knows how to live a limited material life. As soon as my family arrived in Canada, we dug up our backyard and planted a garden where we grew spinach, Swiss chard, onions, and other vegetables. I was taught at a young age how to darn socks on a wonderful little machine, almost a miniature loom that you could place over a wooden dowel.

During the war we saved the silver paper from inside my father's cigarette packages. You took the silver paper off the thin tissue, and made it as tiny as possible by folding it and then scrunching it up. You would wrap the next sheet around that little ball of silver and on and on. We were encouraged to bring them to school where they would be weighed. Our names went up on a chart, depending on how much silver/lead we were giving to the war cause. We also brought in all our wire hangers, and they presumably went to the war cause as well.

My mother made virtually all my clothes and was a very fine seamstress. She had a flair for design and enjoyed sewing. She even continued making me wonderful evening dresses when I was at university. The only items of clothing we bought were winter coats. Luckily our public schools taught all us girls how to sew, and I graduated to a sewing machine in grade eight when I made myself two summer dresses during the spring term. From then on I made a number of outfits from Butterick or Simplicity patterns. My mother and I outfitted me completely for my first year at university.

I learned to knit when I was about seven, and my mother and I made socks for my father and brother. I remember the triumph I felt when I was able to turn a heel for the first time. I don't think we thought of this as being frugal; everybody knitted socks. It just happened that my mother was better at it than most people.

LEARNING HOW TO MANAGE YOUR MONEY

A couple of years ago, I treated myself to an organizer. My friend Esther Giroux is a pro. I've never seen anything like it. Her house is perfectly organized without being irritating; it looks lived in and comfortable. So I hired her to come and help me figure out why my life was an uncontrollable mess. I had no idea just how disorganized my house was. I thought my kids had made the house that way, but when they left home and the mess was still there, I finally had to take the blame.

I am a clutterbug who looks at a pile of junk and cannot sort out how to bring it into some kind of order. I might just nibble at the edges with no design in mind. I would never approach a garden this way, so it baffles me that I'm like this with my house. Maybe it was from my parents' expectation that I be competent and tidy every day of my childhood. Maybe it's a form of rebellion. Alas, it's very discouraging at this great age to realize that I can't be tidy.

Esther spent a day with me, and together we organized my cupboards, drawers, and closets. She made me understand what we were doing and why. We recycled tons of paper (apparently something else, along with clothes, I never throw out), and we moved items into baskets that had labels on them.

It was money well spent. Now I know where things are so I'm not buying the same materials over and over again simply because I cannot find them. The only thing she couldn't fix was my filing: it's still on the floor and all over my desk. It's the way I work and it's never going to change. But here's what organizing did for me:

1. I didn't think I was a materialist, but I had to acknowledge how much stuff I'd accumulated and needed to get rid of. About one-third of the stuff and more than half the paper, went without my really noticing their absence.

2. I stopped buying unnecessary supplies for my plant-consulting business.

3. I stopped buying personal garden supplies; I can actually get along with what I already have.

4. I realized I had to deal with my wardrobe. Saving clothes for forty years is not a good thing.

5. New frugal rule: nothing comes in without something going out.

It's not a big leap from organizing your life to organizing your finances. They go hand in hand. Having a budget and sticking to it means knowing where your money is, just like being organized means opening a drawer and seeing all your pens and pencils in one place. Not knowing how and what you do with your money is the kind of careless-ness that has resulted in a debt-ridden society. You only have to watch a few TV shows about money management to know how easily people can fall into this trap and how eerily similar their stories are.

Saving up to buy something was a natural part of my parents' gen-eration. At that time it was the only way anybody got anything, unless they bartered for it. Then came the layaway plan: you put some money down, the item is put aside for you, and when you make the last pay-ment you get to take it home with you. A new generation is discovering this mode of acquisition. But you cannot go into this agreement brain dead: you are giving up a lot of personal information to join up; there's an automatic deduction from your bank account; and you must understand that those payments have to be made on time. If you default it's game over and you're out of money.

So the first rule of good money management is to never, ever borrow any more than you can afford to pay back. I know way too many people who got trapped by the no-interest credit cards and went into a downward spiral using credit cards to pay off other credit cards to pay off bank loans. One payment missed and you are paying interest on the interest.

The second rule is to consolidate all your debts. Credit cards, student loans, the whole ball of wax ought to be put on one big line of credit. Pay off the interest every month and then sock every cent you can into the principle. If you run into trouble, get to know someone at the bank and let them help you work out your payments. That's what they are in the business of doing: handling money well. But most important is knowing where every penny is going at all times. Believe me, this is not boring. It's rather fun. I have a nice little notebook that I mark every day: how much cash I have, how much is in the bank, how much I owe, and what I need to buy.

The third rule is figuring out your net worth: everything you own, less everything you owe. You may not be as poor as you think. Get your credit rating and see what kind of shape you are in. Pre-authorize all your important bills and deduct them from your bank balance at the

THE ULTIMO THRIFTY CITIZEN

Judy Brunsek is one of the most dynamic people I've ever met. She was downsized from a job she loved in publishing and was devastated. Here's her story.

One of the biggest changes I've made since being laid off was to adopt my mother's model of thrift: if you don't have the money for it, don't buy it. Before I lost my job I was quite a shopaholic and would buy things as retail therapy. My mother — who was widowed with three kids between the ages of eleven and fourteen — never bought anything, other than a house, that she hadn't saved up for. She bought several cars and paid cash for them (she also took care of them like you wouldn't believe — my brother is still driving her spotless and low-kilometre 1992 Protege). She bought herself art, fine china, a fur coat, and kept a household running and maintained — all on a working-class hairdresser's pay and tips. That delayed gratification is something we seldom see these days. She understood that some things were worth more than others and was willing to save up for them instead of frittering her money away.

Now when I want something, I really think about the difference between want and need, price and value, and what the item will or won't bring to my life. I don't think I would have a clue how to do that if I didn't have my mother as a model.

beginning of each month. This sets you on your way to a proper budget. Some day you might want to retire.

The fourth rule of good money management is to become money literate. My personal history with stockbrokers has been terrible. Back in the 1970s, my husband and I gave all our money to a stockbroker, who not only lost it on stupid investments but borrowed more for his daughter's lavish bat mitzvah and never paid it back (alas, he did not spend enough time in jail for other misdemeanours). We weren't tracking our investments; we were money blind, savings stupid. We assumed that an expert would take care of our money, knowing that it was everything we had and we'd be needing it to retire on. I learned the hard way that if people are experts they can be just as dastardly, unethical, and dumb as your average criminal. I also learned to always be aware of exactly what's happening to my money at all times and to manage it myself. Never say to yourself: "I don't understand this money stuff, I'll leave it to someone who does." That's one of the most dangerous thoughts you can have.

👫

There are hundreds of books and newsletters about money management. So educate yourself on how to save and what to spend — which brings me to the next step in becoming a thrifty citizen.

ON BECOMING A BARGAIN HUNTER: THE ART OF HAGGLING

Bargains have always been important in my life. We lived for bargains — it was a triumph of sensible shopping, and being sensible was drummed into me. There are times when I want to say, "Oh, to hell with it, so this isn't the best possible price. So what?" But most of the time I really do like to shop around, look for the best deal, and make sure the cost of the item fits my budget.

Janice Lindsay is a friend, colour consultant, designer, and all-around great shopper. When we discussed the basics of shopping, she made up the following list of rules. They are timeless and important, and I agree with every point. I have tried to live by them, not always flawlessly, but they are terrific guidelines.

1. Do your research.
2. Buy well and you buy once.
3. Thrift is not about cost but about value. To buy a few good pieces that last forever is more thrifty than a bunch of mediocre stuff bought on sale that either wears out or never looks or feels great.
4. Trust your instincts and don't let others boss you around — especially experts.
5. To be a sensible thrifty shopper, don't buy big purchases on the spot. Ask the store to hold things overnight for you. If you wake up with the same frisson of desire you had the day before, get the item. We don't regret what we buy (we can eventually justify anything), but we don't get over the piece we loved that got away.

Haggling is also a fine habit of thrifty citizens and central to many cultures. It's a way of being in serious touch with other people, getting a good deal for yourself, and having some fun. I came from a culture where you never haggled. The price was the price. Naturally, the first time I haggled was strictly an accident.

I was heading for the airport in some Caribbean country when I saw a guy selling huge woven baskets. I just smiled. He lowered the price. I said I wasn't interested. He lowered the price again. Finally, it got so mind-bogglingly cheap, I bought a basket, threw it on top of our luggage, and thought it would never get through customs or survive the trip. It spewed out of the luggage chaos in perfect condition, and we used it for years as the laundry basket.

Talin Vartanian, the CBC's Citizen Talin: Investigative Shopper, is Armenian and haggling is a part of her culture. She says, "People who aren't used to haggling want to fall into a hole in the floor when they shop with me. But so what, all they can do is say no."

She has always been a comparison shopper, especially for big-ticket items. But she doesn't buy because things are cheap. "My parents' basement is full of toilet paper, paper towels, and soap, enough to last all of us for years. They can't stop buying bargains. Whereas I'll see things on sale and stock up, but I won't buy more than I can use in a set amount of time."

What defines a bargain for Talin is buying something at the best possible price but being judicious about where to do it. For instance, she says, "I don't bargain with artisans. I've watched people do this, even those for whom money isn't an issue, and it makes me cringe. But I do think you have to be careful about who you push and how you push. It is not beneath me to bargain in a department store. Sometimes a clerk can and will give you an additional discount."

Making those kinds of distinctions seems right to me. I could never bargain with an artist, let alone an artisan. I spent years working in an art gallery and watched incredibly wealthy people haggle over prices all the time — with people who had nothing except their talent. It left a really bad taste in my mouth. I didn't think I had the right to bargain, but now it seems endemic. And as Talin says, "They can only say no."

The thrifty citizen is one who isn't drowning in stuff. This person is a really good money manager. They pay their debts off and save money on the side, no matter how minuscule the amount, for something wonderful in the future, whether it's a trip, time off, or for retirement.

Now, let's look into the nitty-gritty of our thrifty citizens' lives: what they wear, how they manage their homes and gardens, and how they eat well and travel the world — all within their means. They have a lot to tell us about living the frugal life with style.

CHAPTER 2

THE FRUGAL
FASHIONISTA

I didn't realize I was a frugal dresser until I got to university. When other students saw me wearing the same outfit for the third or fourth week in a row, they got the idea that I didn't have any other clothes. They were pretty close to right. I had several black tops, a couple of then-fashionable voluminous skirts, and not much else. I thought I looked okay, but when people started offering to lend me clothes I made up a story: "My clothes will be here soon, my trunk went astray."

One weekend, I borrowed my aunt's sewing machine and sewed my brains out for three days straight. I ripped apart those gigantic skirts and turned them into slim ones, and made a vest and a stole (which became my signature piece). Everything I had in my meagre closet had to work every which way — mix-and-match was my second name.

And I took to wearing nothing but black. I had been in mourning for my parents for more than a year, so wearing black came naturally to me and I rather liked the look (I was in my Audrey Hepburn period). So for the next two decades, I wore nothing *but* black. I wore so much black I was beginning to feel like a vulture. Eventually, I couldn't stand to look in my closet because I couldn't distinguish one thing from another. I wore black until I realized I was going out and buying the same items I already owned.

Fashionista was not what I was aiming for. Covering my body gracefully was my main goal. And I developed a look. I liked pieces that had a little bit of flair. I discovered capes: they were easy to make, and they cast me as dramatic. Along with black tights, I didn't need a lot more to set me apart.

When I started working, I branched out and went shopping for one good pair of shoes. My first pair of fabulous shoes still haunts me. I adored them, learned to look after them (made friends with a great shoemaker), and wore them for years. Had I known about the cornucopia of second-hand stores (definitely for poor people in those days, and I never considered myself poor), I probably would have been frequenting them. But I didn't discover recycled clothing stores until the 1990s when my then daughter-in-law marched me out for a day of diving into every thrift shop, second-hand store, and recycling depot in the little town we were visiting. And I haven't looked back since.

THE FUNDAMENTALS OF FRUGAL SHOPPING

I learned by observation over the years (and a few spent doing fashion reporting for a national magazine) that there's a big difference between being stylish and being trendy. The latter is what you see young people wearing. And when I was young, I loved trendy: miniskirts couldn't get mini enough for me. But there was a moment somewhere in middle age when being trendy seemed like a major bore.

About the time I could afford it (which tells you something about fashion), I got really interested in classic designs, whether they were by homegrown heroines like Marilyn Brooks or the magnificent Yves Saint Laurent. Changing styles for men and women move with such swiftness it's a real trap for the frugal. But the same assault hits kids a lot harder.

All of our frugal fashion contributors recommended that when you have the need for high quality or a desperate urge for a designer label, shop at high-end department stores for sales. Stock up on basics (underwear, socks, T-shirts) elsewhere. Ask salesclerks for dates, scout flyers, and pay attention to prices before everything goes on sale. You don't want to get whacked for the full price and find it discounted days later. People of all ages told us they never pass up a clearance rack, especially for kids. You can always buy next summer's clothes during the autumn sales.

Online shopping is also an important bargain-hunting tool. But you do have to calculate the cost of exchange, shipping, and duty as you are going through the web sites. Always look for free shipping over a certain amount (unless it's leading you to unnecessary spending). Don't use a credit card online unless the company has a secure system. Even then it's a risk.

The most serious frugal clothing shoppers we talked to, however, wanted to touch the fabric and examine the clothes. Quality is the hallmark of thrifty shopping. And with only a few exceptions these shoppers don't mind haggling, even in a boutique or department store. "Be polite, you can only be turned down" is the mantra. Here are a few bargain-hunting tips from our frugal fashionistas:

- If a clerk can't give you a discount, ask to speak to the manager of the section (go on, be brave), or ask at the cash desk.
- Shop around and mention you've seen the same item at a better price, even if the item you want is already on sale. Retailers want your money and your business. It can't hurt to try.
- Ask for a discount on display items. I recently got 10 percent off a display item, and never looked back.
- Ask for a discount on damaged goods that can be fixed easily and affordably (a sagging hem, a loose or missing button).
- Be sure to check zippers, seams, and buttonholes. If they look ragged, give them a pass because they may be expensive to fix.
- Check out items in the men's and children's departments, which are often much cheaper than women's clothing. Sweatshirts and sweatpants are often a fraction of the cost in the boys' or men's section than in the women's.

⚖ Shop off the beaten track. Look for warehouses out of town, and try to deal direct with manufacturers and wholesalers. Many retailers have a factory shop for discontinued lines where you can get huge savings.

⚖ Shop off-season (buy spring in autumn).

⚖ Hang on to all tags and receipts. If you're having second thoughts about an item you've just purchased, then have no qualms about returning it. Don't hang on to things you hate.

⚖ Ask yourself how much mileage you will get out of an item (how many times, when, and where you can wear it) and spend accordingly.

⚖ Comfort is fundamental. If you do not feel comfortable in a piece of clothing (too tight, too short, itchy, see-through), you probably won't wear it more than once.

Karen Mondok is a mother in a single-income family with four kids twelve years old and under. As she says, searching for bargains on food, primarily, and entertainment, is paramount in their household. She never, ever pays retail for anything. She clips coupons and searches the weekly flyers for the best deals on necessary items. "I shop at used and/or consignment shops for most of my kids' clothing. I am constantly in search of good-quality, good-value entertainment for my family. I value quality of life over possessions. But every household has a splurge threshold." Karen's splurge threshold is buying at least one or two items from a favourite local designer, and once in a while

BEST BARGAIN STORIES

Twenty years ago I bought a long, beautifully designed leather skirt that was very expensive even at half price at a Boxing Day sale. I wore it to death and felt great every time I put it on. When it got too embarrassing to wear it, I put it away. A few years later when I was sorting through my closet, I unearthed it and started wearing it again. Unfortunately, the first time I did, I ended up working on a project with a guy I hadn't seen for years. When I walked in wearing The Skirt, he said: "I can't believe you are still wearing that." Well, I am still wearing it and it was worth every penny. — *Designer and Colour Consultant Janice Lindsay*

My best bargain was buying a long black velvet dress for $5 from a second-hand store that raises money for the local hospital. I also bought some elegant high-heeled black shoes for $2, as I needed both for an evening function. I was thrilled because they both fit perfectly. — *Author and Gardening Columnist Sonia Day*

I don't hunt, exactly. I prowl and pounce when I spy something with pedigree but at a discounted price. I'm not driven to find a particular item. I'm open to the thrill of discovery, so I visit shops often, not with an eye to buying something necessarily, but to see what might be available. Some of my scores include a solid-silver Jensen bangle that I know retails for up to $800 and I purchased for $20 at a consignment store. The bangle was hiding behind some costume pieces. I knew what it was at a glance. I suppose my secret, if I have one, is that I have champagne taste but a beer budget. So I frequent the high-end stores to see what's what and take a mental picture of the quality items so I can recognize them when they are in a much more depressed setting. I suppose it's like antiques hunting in the flea markets of Paris. There's junk, but if you have a honed eye you will spot the one item of value and grab it. — *Fashion Writer Deirdre Kelly* treating her daughter to something retail. "I almost never buy retail for my boys, who prefer gently worn clothing anyway and who have not yet become overly fashion conscious." Her best tips:

- ⚖ Avoid buying excessively trendy clothes that serve only one purpose or occasion.
- ⚖ Search for studio sales. You have to sort through a lot of stuff, but you can end up with excellent-quality clothing.
- ⚖ Find a good tailor or dressmaker to do alterations, as off-the-rack clothing doesn't work for everyone.

And remember: Do not go shopping for clothes until you have a healthy attitude toward your body, a firm grasp on your financial situation, and a finely tuned sense of the difference between your needs and wants. How we shop indicates our state of spiritual and mental health.

WHEN TO SAVE AND WHEN TO SPLURGE

One of the baffling things about liking clothes and looking for them is knowing when you must spend money and when you absolutely must walk away. It goes back to knowing the difference between a want and a need: it's fundamental to your personality. In other words you shouldn't go shopping unless you know yourself very well. Otherwise you are going to spend money foolishly.

Shopping is seductive; it can ravish you with its outpouring of lovely calming feelings, and it can be useful or it can be dangerous. I have a friend who is prone to depression and she works it out shopping, which is a very expensive bit of therapy. If there's a rule of thumb with shopping it's that you don't use it to counteract anger or depression. A long walk in the park is a lot cheaper and far more restorative.

Being confident about your taste is another value to add to being a frugalista. Take Karen von Hahn who writes about the current scene for the *Globe and Mail*. She feels that the height of Cheap Chic is wearing a one-of-a-kind vintage outfit for the evening. She spends serious money on jackets, coats, and shoes, and saves on T-shirts and summer basics by shopping at low-end but fashionable chain stores, teen-oriented mall shops, and ethnic importers. These retailers, along with vintage stores, are where she finds her best bargains.

The Art of Mixing and Matching

One of the most enchanting art functions/fundraisers I've attended is called The Uniform Project. The artist, Sheena Matheiken, is wearing the same dress for a year to raise money for schools in India. It's a well-designed basic black tunic, which can be worn front-to-back and back-to-front. She has such a good sense of herself, her body, and her style that she seems to have no trouble making daily dramatic changes to this simple uniform. The project itself is a gold mine of ideas about how to add frugal accessories (she buys a lot of stuff from thrift stores, flea markets, and on eBay) and put pieces together to give each outfit a contemporary look.

It's important to the thrifty to develop a look and enhance it in small ways that create a major impact. Here are some tips on the art of mixing and matching:

- Combine an inexpensive item like a tank top or a T-shirt with a great jacket or sweater. It's a sophisticated look and stretches your clothing repertoire.

- Reinvent an old look. Remember when *everything* was covered with sequins (après-party cleanup was about vacuuming up sparkles)? Look for something from that era el cheapo and add something classic from this era to give a boring outfit some oomph at night.

- Learn to accessorize. Deborah Fulsang, a fashion writer and consultant, says that for the budget-minded, accessories will give you the most bang for your buck. Fantastic, eccentric, colourful, ornate, or otherwise unique shoes will make you feel sexy, womanly, stylish. And scarves are just about the best accessory you can have. Learn how to use them. Also, crazy tights in loud argyles make a simple black dress pop. Have fun with your accessories, and even your basics will look updated and fresh.

- Buy fun jewellery. Fashion writer Deirdre Kelly has been reporting from Paris and Milan for almost a decade, and she says she gets to know a style and looks for it, whether it's art deco (alas, out of reach now, but once upon a time you could

A FRUGAL FAMILY
By Katherine Ashenburg, Author of *The Dirt on Clean*

Thrift is our middle name, on both sides of my family. My mother used to say that she decided my father was The One when she spotted a brooch across the road when they were out walking, and sent him over to pick it up. He went without a word. She wore the brooch for years.

We all pick things up off the street. My cousin Gary who lives in Rochester, New York, has taken the family penchant to what some (not us) would consider extreme: he is a Dumpster diver and, boy, is there great stuff to be found there. Once he found a whole Talbot's wardrobe, and we picked over it for a long time. My own, less adventurous ways are pretty obvious: I go to second-hand stores in my neighbourhood, and for a while we had one of those buy-by-the-pound shops, where I got several excellent cotton summer shirts.

I believe my mother induced a kind of blindness to non-sale racks in me, in that when I go in a shop I almost literally don't see anything but the rack that says "Reduced" or "On Sale." With difficulty, occasionally, if I really need something, I force myself to look at the regular racks, but I always feel I'm letting my mother down.

The best bargain I ever got was when I bought an off-white, linen, slim wedding dress on sale from $125 to $25 at Rochester's good department store. It was a casual, almost tailored, 1960s-style wedding dress, with a slim skirt and cap sleeves. My grandmother, who did all the family sewing, cut off the cap sleeves and the train, and I wore it to two formal dances at university (which we had in those days). Three years later, I got engaged. What to wear for the wedding? My grandmother held up the cap sleeves triumphantly. The train couldn't be resewn, but she'd been saving the sleeves for just this occasion. And that's what I wore on my wedding day, with a little daisy wreath.

find this stuff everywhere); art moderne (a little less expensive), or Victorian. Ditto to a marvellous piece of costume jewellery, be it a cocktail ring, shoulder-dusting crystal-encrusted earrings, or stacks and stacks of bangles.

My friend Carol Cowan is an amazing shopper, the kind of person who can go into Zen mode walking into a huge discount store and keep an open mind. Her take on designer clothes: "While I like to dress well, my feelings of self-worth are not tied to wearing instantly recognizable fashion items. But I do sometimes buy expensive clothing: my favourite form of 'rationalization' is to amortize the cost of an item over the number of years I might wear it. If I buy an expensive winter coat, by the time I've convinced myself I'll be wearing it for the next five years, the cost always seems manageable, negligible, or downright thrifty."

THRIFT STORE SHOPPING

Thrift stores, consignment shops, vintage boutiques: give them any name you want, the world of used clothing is everywhere once you start looking. The pioneer of second-hand fashion in my life is Sheree-Lee Olson. Sheree-Lee is the Style editor of the *Globe and Mail*, and she always looks like a million bucks. Her thrift store shopping habits were a serious revelation to me. She took me to church rummage sales, the Salvation Army, professional second-hand shops, upscale, downscale, she knows them all.

Her thrift-shop days began when she was an art student on a fixed budget. "I had no money then but I had time," she says. "I would spend three to four hours on a Saturday afternoon, exploring every thrift shop and liquidation centre in my neighbourhood, looking for something cool to wear. There were lots of parties at art school, and we were definitely competitive about who had the best clothes. So when I found a black-and-white op-art 1960s sheath for six bucks, it made me very happy."

Sheree-Lee thinks there is something beyond straight economics going on here: "I like the idea of thrift shopping as a kind of historiography. On a cultural level, it's like the old bridal formula for the wedding dress: 'something old, something new, something borrowed, something blue.' We accept history and symbolism when it's connected to our ceremonial garments, but the idea of wearing something handed down — even if it's from a relative — used to be off-putting for many people. When I grew up, everyone wanted shiny and new.

"Of course, once 'used' or 'second-hand' was rebranded 'vintage' — and especially once Hollywood actresses started wearing vintage on the red carpet — everything changed. My grandmother would have loved the trend. She had some great dresses from the 1950s — not labels, she was a woman who worked as a salesclerk all her life at a department store. She knew I loved vintage clothes, and sent me a couple of boxes of dresses before she died. When I wore those dresses to parties, I felt I was honouring her — as well as trumping every other woman in the room. People liked the fact that there was a story behind each piece — one dress I wore a lot was the dress my grandmother wore to my parents' wedding.

"My grandmother was also a great circulator of culture herself. She would pick up paintings and postcards at rummage sales; she had a kind of curator's eye, and she enjoyed speculating about the stuff. So when I began to devote a lot of time to thrift store shopping, I was always aware that there were stories behind that crocheted blanket or those hand-painted bowls. I would take them home and give them a second life.

"I stopped thrift shopping as much when I got a full-time job, and I had more money and less time. But I went back to it in a big way when my kids were small. Kids go through tons of clothes, and often the stuff you find at second-hand stores has barely been worn. Whereas at art school I was shopping mostly for entertainment value, for my kids I was shopping for quality. I started paying more attention to fabrics — "hand feel" in fashion parlance — and natural fibres. People pour a lot of love into the clothes they make for children, and I found little hand-knit sweaters with bunnies and little hats with pom-poms that were some of the sweetest things my kids wore.

"For little kids, especially, my friend Iris says used clothes are in a sense better than new. They've been broken in. Her kids were fussy and liked only soft fabrics against their skin. Buying used meant the fabric had revealed its true nature, what it was like after ten or even fifty washings. This was a new perspective for me, and what it revealed was the notion of inherent quality. High-quality cotton fleeces don't pill; they get softer and more comfortable with age."

Sheree-Lee got rid of my prejudice about used clothing many years ago. Now my closet is filled with masses of other people's stuff rejigged for my own life: shirts, jackets (always a great thing to look for), vests, and scarves. I can now venture out confidently on my own, and I'm developing a pretty good eye. But it requires a bit of skill and a lot of practice. Here are a few tips on how to shop in a thrift store, gathered from those who know:

- ⚰ Take your time. Bring your iPod and get into a shopping groove.
- ⚰ Don't expect to find exactly what you are looking for.
- ⚰ Always look at shoes and purses first.
- ⚰ If you pick up an item for more than three seconds, try it on — there is always a reason something catches your eye.
- ⚰ Never buy anything that looks like something you already have.
- ⚰ Make sure what you buy is well made. Always check that the material is of good quality.
- ⚰ Thrift shops have sales. Look for the discounted aisles where you'll find almost illegal steals.
- ⚰ Examine each item meticulously, looking for holes, stains, broken or missing buttons. Think first, "Why did someone get rid of such a wonderful item?," and eliminate it if you think it was because it hangs wrong or is beyond repair.
- ⚰ Try the item on and walk around in it to make sure it fits, looks good, and makes you feel wow. Thrift stores usually don't allow for returns or exchanges.
- ⚰ Look in the consignment stores where wealthy and stylish women regularly dump their perfectly good clothes. These

are clients who are up-to-the minute fabulous, and feel no compunction purging their closets once or twice yearly to get new seasonal clothes.

⚐ If you *need* a new winter coat, don't buy four pairs of black pants because they are a bargain.

⚐ If you must (though we were advised by everyone to go it alone), go with one experienced person (but not after lunch and a glass of wine) and watch how he or she shops.

⚐ Don't get seduced by prices alone.

⚐ Ask what days the outlet receives new stock and make a point of getting there midday when they've had time to add new items on the floor.

⚐ My doctor recommends that anything you buy in a second-hand store should be dry cleaned immediately.

If you find a good consignment or thrift shop, make yourself known and go regularly. Eventually, the staff will get to know your taste and will be setting pieces aside for you. The thrift store culture is worth understanding and getting to know, even if it takes a little bit of time and energy.

EXTENDING AND MAINTAINING
A FRUGAL WARDROBE

Wardrobe upkeep is just as important as paying attention to all parts of your house. Well-made clothes will last for years. To be truly frugal, give up all thoughts of throwing out (or giving away or selling) clothing

THRIFT STORE SHOPPING FOR MEN

My husband, author Jack Batten, is one of the sharpest dressers I know. When I asked him about his sartorial splendour, this is what he wrote:

Women always ask about my brown Harris tweed jacket. Older woman say it's the kind of thing their husbands would love to wear. Younger women say, "Ooh, that's so cool. Who designed it?" People of all ages ask how much it cost. A fortune, they suppose.

"No," I answer smugly, "I paid $14 for my authentic brown Harris tweed."

I got the jacket at a second-hand clothing store called Value Village. Toronto, where I live, has five Value Village outlets, each one the size of a warehouse and with huge parking lots. But many cities have the same kind of retail stores, specializing in clothes passed along by the original owners and sold at spectacular discounts.

The Harris tweed isn't the only jacket I've picked up at Value Village. My second jacket is black, chic, and cut in the Italian style. I may be guessing about the jacket's origins, but the label says it's a Missoni and in smaller letters under Missoni is the word "Italy." Would they fib about a thing like that?

Value Village is divided into men's and women's sections, then the gender sections are divided by the type of clothes: jackets in two rows, shirts in two more, then sweaters and trousers and windbreakers in their own places.

Personally, I've had my best luck with jackets and shirts. In shirts, all priced at no more than six bucks, I've got a Ralph Lauren, a Holt Renfrew, an Arrow, and an Yves, though it may not be Saint Laurent. The Yves and all the others fit me just right, which is something I can't say for my two pairs of Value Village trousers. Both hang on me so unnaturally that I've stopped wearing them. I'm thinking of selling them back to Value Village.

Except for the ill-hanging trousers, all of my cheap stuff doesn't look at all cheap. I feel confident wearing them in any social situation, and I like the feeling that I'm saving serious money on clothes.

As for shoes, I buy in women's shoe stores during sales. My feet happen to be small, a size seven at most, and women's shoes fit me perfectly. It takes someone with a very keen eye for shoes, almost always a woman, to spot my bisexual footwear. Not that I feel uneasy about getting outed. Besides, two factors balance out any possible embarrassment: one is that women's shoes — flats, of course — offer more variety in design; and, second, for some reason unfathomable to me, the discount at women's shoe sales is much larger than at men's shoe sales. And saving money, after all, is what the exercise is all about.

after only a few uses. Turn your mind to looking after high-quality garments, from storing your clothes, to making repairs, to reinventing an old look entirely.

Storing Clothes

Margaret Atwood has turned storing clothes into an art. Here are her invaluable tips:

1. Wash clothes before storing. Moths live on organic matter. They love wool and are much more likely to eat a wool sweater with a lot of lanolin or sweat in it than any other kind.
2. Then, freeze your clothes for about three days, unfreeze them, and then freeze them again. This process will kill the larvae.

3. After you've carefully dried your clothing (to avoid mildew), store immediately.

4. Buy an airtight metal trunk with cedar lining. You can still find them at army surplus stores. If the air can't get in, the moths can't live. They can only eat their way through plastic, or anything porous. The much-advertised containers that suck air out with a vacuum are okay, but they don't last very long.

5. Vacuum out all the frass (moth feces, which has the consistency of fine sand).

6. Purchase moth detectors, which don't kill the insects but let you know if you've got any. Change them every three months.

We often don't think about how we store clothes, but if your attitude is one of longevity, the more good storage you have the more likely you'll be pulling these items out for another go-around for seasons to come.

Clothing Upkeep

Though we are surrounded by what appears to be a disposable society, we also have people all around us who can repair, refit, and recycle good fabrics and clothing. It doesn't take that much time to become a careful handler of clothes, and the payoff is astounding. Here are a few tips on clothing upkeep:

△ Learn to sew. Back in the 1950s my mother was expecting to get a black negligee from my father for her birthday. Instead, he gave her the very first portable Singer sewing machine. She may have been crushed by the practicality of his gift, but I still use it today.

⚘ If you've got a jacket or coat that looks pathetic, give it a good wash, hang it out in the sun (great for taking out stains), and add new buttons.

⚘ Make sure you have a really good shoe-repair person in your life. He or she can make a good pair of shoes last for years.

⚘ If you have scuffed shoes, put a tiny bit of Vaseline or hand lotion on a soft cloth and rub it into the shoe for an instant shine with no polish.

⚘ If you find the perfect outfit and it doesn't quite fit, take it to a tailor.

What keeps a frugal fashionista going is not only having items in the closet that you love, but the length of time you've owned them and what memories they bring. I never view wearing the same outfit over and over again as a fault or a lacking in imagination. Every time I wear a particular outfit another memory of when I wore it will shoot forward. If it's not a good one, it might produce a "This time things will be fabulous" feeling. And that there is what I call retail therapy.

SWAP AND SELL

I was convinced for many decades that all the superb outfits I'd saved from the 1960s would eventually be donated to the local museum (nope). By the time I found out they were not collector's items, I was much too attached to get rid of them. Going through my closet is almost like shopping: endorphins flutter by as I sift through my lovely past. But when we pack rats can be corralled into admitting that we aren't actually going to wear those size-1 jeans ever again, the next step is to host a swap party or sell your unwanted clothes.

A Swap Party

To organize a swap party, make sure your shopping buddies understand the rules: potluck, BYOB, and the clothes have to be clean and mended. Get a glass of wine into everyone's hands first, read the rules, and go to it:

1. Place everything in one spot so rummaging is fun and easy.
2. Draw a number and go in order (lowest number to highest or vice versa).
3. Choose one item at a time until the pile has run out.
4. Swapping items within the group afterward is allowed. Being petty is not.

You might pick up something pretty nice, but even better, you get rid of stuff from your own closet and know it will be well used. One of the fundamentals of being frugal is also being organized. You can't live with a stuffed closet and go out and get more things. Remember the frugal motto: one item comes in, one goes out.

A Family Fair

Here's another idea on how to clear out the closet: invite all the members of your family over. Tell them to bring bags. Display everything you can bear to get rid of in an artistic way and then let them go crazy. It keeps the clothing in the family and occasionally you get to visit your stuff.

A Gold Party

Another kind of party that is building a following is a gold party. You invite an appraiser to one person's house, and the guests bring all their unwanted gold. Everyone takes a number, the jeweller examines the piece, and then makes an offer. The average total of sales to guests is $10,000, and the host gets to keep a percentage of the sales. The gold itself is melted down to make new jewellery. Certainly brings you back to the needs versus wants.

Selling Your Clothes

Though my black-ridden closet was boring to me, it was also filled with treasures I can no longer wear due to the fact that they are smaller than I ever remember being. I decided to take some garments to various shops, starting with the high-end boutiques and working my way to the vintage (if you are convinced that your old ball gown is true vintage — which means it's more than twenty years old — go there first). The rest went to charities. To sell, you must fuss: dry clean, mend, and offer clothing in good condition.

THE BEAUTY BUSINESS

Beauty products can cost the earth, but many years ago my dermatologist steered me clear of expensive high-end products and toward more economical ones. They do the same job. My mother used Pond's cold cream all her short life and had glorious skin. The Body Shop used to have a great night cream, but when they were bought by L'Oréal they added perfume to the product and I had to find something new. The market servicing those who need non-scented goods is getting better, but once again you have to do your research. Sometimes chemicals are used to take out the chemical smells.

Many of our contributors consider their health and diet regime their beauty program. Most of them are vegetarians and a few are vegans. My computer techie, twenty-four-year-old Koko Karunathan, says, "Being informed is the most important thing. I try not to buy into the glitz and 'lifestyle' of high-end stores. Most of their products are sold at pharmacies; shiny lights and jazzy music has no effect on the product or my health." Here are some useful tips on how to save and where to spend on beauty products:

- ⚖ Use natural/homemade skin treatments, and check out YouTube and Treehugger for their tutorials and reviews of organic products.
- ⚖ Keep an eye out for sales and buy multiples of products (shampoo, deodorant) when they are at half price.

- Use baby wipes with a little eye-makeup remover to take off makeup.
- Use a face cloth instead of spending money on cotton balls.

I love looking at beauty ads to get ideas about what's going on in the world of makeup. But I've scaled down my needs to a few basics: face wash, eye-makeup remover, night cream, face cream. Makeup is another one of those items where you get what you pay for. I always ask people who look great what they are wearing; it saves me from spending money on products I may not like. And every once in a while someone will recommend a real bargain product and I buy.

Hair Salons and Spas

Hair salons and spas are wonderful services to indulge in, but they can be costly. If you want to get a really inexpensive haircut, the big salons, such as Aveda or Vidal Sassoon, offer affordable haircuts from students-in-training. They take a long time to cut, you'll get something pretty interesting, and you won't spend a lot of money. Be sure to tip them well — they may be students, but they also need to earn a living.

Some of our contributors frequent cheap salons for a trim, or snip off the ends of their hair at home. Then they save up for a serious cut in a real salon.

I've long since settled on my clothing style, as well as hair and makeup. Once you have some confidence in yourself, you don't really need to have the latest crimp or drape. The great thing about fashion is that it has become so much fun. And in the end what you wear should make you feel wonderful, no matter where you shop for your clothes.

CHAPTER 3

THE FRUGAL
FOODIE

I f there is a defining element in understanding the difference between cheap and frugal, it's food. Over and over again our thrifty contributors said that when it comes to food, they are never, ever cheap. The thrifty of this world agree that quality is essential when it comes to what we put in our bodies.

In my parents' home, no matter what the circumstances, we always ate well. We adored food. Each meal was a major gathering time, and leftovers were almost unheard of because you were never given much more than you could eat. If there was anything left on a plate, another kid would happily polish it off.

We knew what to expect as well: the roast was served at noon on Sunday (sandwiches for supper in the evening); Sunday leftovers on Monday; shepherd's pie on Tuesday; chili on Wednesday; liver on Thursday; fish and chips on Friday; and oxtail stew on Saturday. This cycle is engraved in my mind. We ate beef because it was affordable and it was easily available, and I learned then to love all the cheap cuts of meat, such as the tongue, liver, and tail. I still make a great oxtail stew.

But my special memories are from the time we went to our cottage near St. Pierre de Wakefield, Quebec. We picked up fresh produce from farmhouses on the way to the lake, and my mother cooked the most astonishing and delicious meals on a wood stove. Were baby carrots ever so glorious? Potatoes cooked with mint and fresh butter ever as exquisite? Was there a dream so divine as thick cream drowning raspberries warm from the sun? If we needed fish we'd go out and catch some. I can whip up an appetite just coasting on memories.

I've been attempting to replicate those simple, delicious meals ever since, and buy vegetables grown as close to home as possible. My mother was smart enough to make sure I knew how to cook and bake pies, tarts, brownies, and all the other sweets the family adored.

I don't remember us ever *not* being on a very tight budget. We simply couldn't afford prepared food when it was introduced, and I never developed a taste for it. If we needed a hit of french fries, Mum made a batch. But here's the huge difference from my parents' home and my own: there were never any leftovers. Now I seem to be battling the green monsters all the time.

As a young mother, I learned pretty early on that I would find my best food bargains in ethnic stores. And it helped that we lived in a well-serviced neighbourhood. Though I was budget conscious, we started eating organic food during the 1960s, when I was working on a story about the movement for a national magazine. It certainly turned me into a believer, and I got used to the idea that I would always be paying more for high-quality, nutritious food. The result of this habit is that you buy less and compost any scraps so it keeps moving on.

I'm not sure if we ran a frugal home when there were just two kids bounding around. But once I remarried and had a weekend-blended family, things changed dramatically. With four kids eating non-stop, I seemed to be either shopping or cooking all the time. I organized what we'd eat during the week and have some sort of vague food cycle on the go. Like most mothers I'd cook what the kids liked, mainly to avoid food fights. I'll never forget the day I served a steak for the first time in months, only to have one of the kids look at it and say: "I'm a vegetarian."

No one tells you how much work four kids are, let alone how much they eat and what they do to a house, no matter how well raised they are. But once I got the house reorganized, I got to thinking very carefully about the relationship between shopping, cooking, and money.

FOODIE ON A PENSION

One person whose style of living I've been fascinated by over the years is my friend Juliet Mannock. She's a stellar gardener who loves to read, eat, and cook. She's on a strict pension, but she entertains several times a year on a biggish scale, has friends over for tea, and whips together treats for herself at a moment's notice. Juliet does not believe in mammoth sizes of anything, especially when living on a small budget.

I grew up in World War II and learned to turn off the lights in empty rooms and generally loathe any kind of waste. I rarely throw out food because I almost never buy more than enough to last three meals or one week. I hate reheated leftovers, ditto frozen entrées. I buy only seasonal fruit and veg, and if this means no tomatoes from November to May when the hydroponics appear, so be it. Fresh food tastes delicious and is bursting with nutritional value.

I buy red meat perhaps once a month or less, chicken two to three times a month. Luckily, I don't like rich food, so I stick to a diet that relies on porridge, eggs, milk, fish, margarine, olive oil, cheeses, fresh artisanal bread made with local flours, and pasta. Treats for me are liverwurst on toast, shrimp, smoked salmon, champagne, and a smooth Amontillado sherry.

A MEAL PLAN

Here's what I learned shopping for what seemed like a horde at the time, our family of six: you have to have a PLAN. My plan was unvaried until the kids grew into gigantic teenagers who didn't stop eating for about four years. They always complained there was nothing to eat, even though the fridge was full of fruit and vegetables. The rule was: if you want a snack, have an apple or a carrot.

But I stuck to my guns with the food plan. I got sick of cooking the same old same old, but they adored my food and it was my way of showing the deep love I held for them. A food plan makes life so much easier because you know what you'll be eating on any given day. I cooked in bulk on the weekend and froze what we weren't going to eat. We had chicken at least twice a week, red meat once a week, plus chili. It's not as boring as it seems, since there are always seasonal changes in vegetables to add to the protein.

SHOPPING FOR FOOD

Our frugal foodies spoke loud and clear: they cook from scratch; they buy only what's in season; and they usually eat meat, at most, a couple of times a week. They do not buy snacks or pre-prepared foods, and many do their own baking.

Eating meat has turned into a conundrum for most of us. No one recommended eating it every day. In fact, most of our contributors ate meat a few times a month and then only very high-quality stuff. They

FOOD GROUPS

Our attitudes toward and relationship with food is often formed by how our parents approached nutrition when we were young. My friend Uli Haverman is that impressive combination of thoughtfulness, smarts, and frugality. She explains her history with food.

My parents were immigrants from a destroyed Germany where they endured many years of "starvation" (as my mother puts it), as food was scarce to nonexistent. They instilled in me the notion of survival. One does whatever is necessary to stay healthy and strong.

So I always break down food into their nutritional groups, protein being the most important. I will eat a protein, or I will eat a grain or a vegetable/fruit in no particular order or combination, as long as I eat some of each during the day. When I go to a restaurant (even my kids have been trained to do this), I always eat the protein first since it's the most expensive item in the meal. That way, if I'm full, my body has taken in the most valuable nutrient and the expense of the other items is minimized.

During the months when I work outside of the house, I eat oatmeal every day for lunch. It is quick, filling, and inexpensive. I am capable of preparing a traditional meal, and all the meals I have prepared have been met with rave reviews, but I rarely do the cooking. Since I don't live alone, I try to keep certain staples in the pantry so that anyone can put a meal together quickly and easily. I can make anything with flour, sugar, eggs, milk, and butter. My best advice for saving money on food is to make everything from scratch and use the purest forms of food available.

bought a lot of organic chicken. They also ate lots of beans (lentils, black, navy, and white) and purchased them in bulk in health food or ethnic stores, or scouted out such places in strip malls — you never know where you'll turn up a food bargain.

When it comes to shopping for food, the first rule is never step into a supermarket without a list, or you will end up buying things you a) don't need; and b) aren't part of The Plan and therefore beyond The Budget. Supermarkets are designed to *make* you shop. The milk is situated at the back of the store so you have to trawl through all those other goodies to get a litre or two. Produce is in one place, and meat is in another. In between are tempting treats begging to be bought and devoured the minute you get home.

Second, read the weekly specials, but don't buy simply for the savings. If they are selling off roasts, maybe it is a good idea to buy a few and stockpile them. Or if there's a sale on your favourite brand of butter, for instance, you may want to buy several pounds and freeze it. But don't get sucked into buying too much; you may purchase items you won't end up consuming, which results in waste — of time, money, and food.

This is a shopping plan that has worked for me over the years:

1. Have a basic shopping list before you go to the store and stick to it. Divide it into supermarket, ethnic shops, and farmers' markets. Make sure to look at what you already have in stock.

2.   Never shop before lunch. You'll be starving and everything will look great.

3.   Have a budget. Figure out how much money you can afford for food, then divide it by the number of meals you have to serve in a week. You can sort out how much you've got to spend on each meal. I had a little wallet strictly for food money. When the money was gone, it was gone. I also keep a specific amount of cash in my handbag for shopping at farmers' markets. Same rule applies: when the money's gone, it's gone.

4.   Buy cheaper cuts of meat, which have the same nutritional value as the more expensive cuts, and buy less. Bulk your meal up with vegetables and beans.

5.   Don't buy more than you can fit into the cupboard or fridge.

6.   Do not buy prepared foods or snacks. They are a waste of money, and are full of salt, oil, and sugar. It is unbelievably bad for our bodies, and the kids will pay for it for the rest of their lives.

7.   Make rules about junk food: tell the kids they need to save up for it and buy it with their own money.

8.   Don't fill the fridge with tempting prepackaged casseroles. They are expensive on a per-person serving. Instead, have healthy emergency meals on hand, such as a really good frozen meat loaf (hot one night, sandwiches the next day for lunch).

Here are some more great tips from our master foodies on what to look for when shopping for groceries:

✕ Shop for meat at the best place you can find. There are butchers that carry organic chickens and meat from animals slaughtered in a humane way. They cost the earth so don't buy a lot.

✕ Buy extra meat when it's on sale, and freeze it in individual portions. Boneless chicken breasts and pork chops always go on sale eventually, and often at half price. But make sure not to over-stock, and always remember to use what you have purchased before buying more.

✕ Go to specialty stores for specialty items: a high-end market for vanilla extract, a good bakery for bread, a cheese store for cheese.

✕ Check out supermarkets and big-box stores for laundry detergent and canned goods.

✕ Organic food may cost a lot, but it's the best thing we can do for ourselves and the environment.

✕ Travel to shop. Visit two or three specialty shops at once. Chinatown is a great place for the frugal shopper.

✕ Share your garden with neighbours (your zucchinis for their tomatoes).

✕ If you buy in bulk or by the case, share it with somebody and split the costs in half.

✕ Make sure you are buying the freshest items available, especially if you know you want them to last for a few weeks.

✕ Be careful with fish: if they are piled skin on top of flesh, bacteria can contaminate them. They should not be stacked, or if so, it's flesh to flesh, skin to skin.

It still saddens me when I think about how I used to resent all the time it took to shop for food. I realize now it's one of the more important elements of our daily lives. Now, every foray seems like an exquisite adventure. Attitude has a lot to do with how you feel about food and the way you spend your time on it. If you are having trouble with shopping for food or you feel you just don't have the time, maybe now's the moment for you to analyze why you feel this way. Think about it.

Coupons

Coupons have become newly fashionable. You know something is up when you have a friend who never in her life used a coupon and is now bragging about her savings. My friend Lynda flummoxed me completely when she said she had started coupon clipping: "For the first time a couple of weeks ago, I sent away for coupons from Proctor & Gamble's web site, and now I get $3 off my Oral B replacement toothbrush and $2 off Venus disposable shavers. I also always buy Tropicana orange juice because you get ten air mile points. Quaker Wheaties gets you twenty-five. The point is, more people are using coupons. I see it all the time so I'm starting. It's fun to think of the bargains you're getting."

There are dozens and dozens of coupon web sites, but be forewarned: most of them blitz you with a lot of advertising. And time is an element here, so there are a couple of things to know. Here's Citizen Talin's advice:

- X Keep only the coupons for items you buy all the time.
- X Organize your coupons in a drawer.
- X Don't buy an item just because you have a coupon for it.
- X If you spot a two-for-one deal and you have two coupons for a dollar off, you can use both coupons. So if you see an item that's buy two for $3 (or buy one, get one free), then slap down your two coupons and you should get each one for a buck.

When I asked Talin if she had a special way of organizing her coupons, she admits that, like most of us, she just tosses them in a drawer and has to fish for them. But serious coupon collectors have little wallets with a best-before-date filing system, and check the web sites constantly. You can also trade coupons, which means you grab every one you can, then go online and look for the ones you need, mail them to the person who needs yours, and so on. There's no shortage of savings to be had.

THE FRUGAL PANTRY AND FRIDGE

One time I was cleaning out the fridge and found rolls of film that had been stored there since before the invention of digital cameras — apparently, I wasn't moving things around fast enough. If you tidy up the fridge on a regular basis, you'll use up what you have, buy fewer items, and keep them around for a shorter length of time. The temptation is to buy anything on sale, but it ends up cluttering the pantry and, more often than not, going to waste. Only buy stuff that you know you will use again and again.

I'm a collector of olive oils and have a minimum of five types on the go, plus vegetable oil for high-heat cooking, and small jars of mayo (they take up less room) because the gigantic ones go out of date quickly. The whole idea of using what you have is a frugal mantra. Here are absolutes in my fridge: capers, mint sauce, light soy, cranberry chutney, homemade chili sauce, Patak's curry sauce, and *fleur de sel*. But I wanted to find out what serious cooks have in their fridges and pantries, and here's what they have to say.

A Chef's Pantry and Refrigerator

Chef Esther Benaim of Great Cooks on Eight (both a cooking school and restaurant) was forced to re-evaluate her kitchen basics when her son returned home. She came up with the following list:

- ✕ Beans
- ✕ Coconut milk
- ✕ Spices
- ✕ Flour
- ✕ Nutella
- ✕ Almond butter (a staple for a snack instead of peanut butter)

X Crackers, especially rice crackers

X Sauces from the country of origin: Chinese sauces (oyster sauce, soy, hot sauce); Thai (peanut sauce); Japanese (wasabi); Italian; Vietnamese fish sauce.

X Three to four different mustards

X Sesame oil

X Vinegars

X Olive oil

X Salts

A Baker's Pantry

Uli Haverman is one of the best bakers I've ever come across. Here are her essentials:

X Unbleached flour

X White sugar

X Dark brown sugar

X Demerara sugar

X Eggs

X Butter

X Canola oil

X Large-flake oats

X Raisins

X Chocolate chips

✕ The best vanilla and almond extracts
✕ Jars of sour cherries
✕ Tins of peach halves
✕ Bricks of cream cheese
✕ Sour cream
✕ Oreo crumbs and graham cracker crumbs
✕ Cornstarch
✕ Lots of apples

What's in the fridge and pantry should be culled on a regular basis. It's surprising how many meals can be concocted without ever leaving the house, particularly when dealing with leftovers. It takes only a little time and creativity to put the two together.

REDUCE, REUSE, RECYCLE: THE ART OF LEFTOVERS

There is something really disturbing about our disposable society. It is shocking how much garbage even small families produce. We have rules that make it necessary to throw out all sorts of good food in restaurants, and we carry this attitude of contempt for leftover food into our own homes. Who would consider serving a meal of leftovers to guests?

I was amused to see a work of conceptual art recently where everything was cooked so that it *looked* like leftovers. If artists see this as an issue, we frugal foodies must take control of our food ever more aggressively. And with some imagination and creativity, all the great cooks do.

Esther Benaim says she takes leftover food home from a cooking class or the restaurant and will reinvent it. Here are some of her ideas, as well as tips from our other frugal foodies:

X Leftover vegetables make a good omelette or frittata, especially potatoes.

X A little leftover hamburger can make a fantastic spaghetti sauce.

X Chop up half a leftover lobster, add an egg, chives, tarragon, and orange pepper, form them into small patties, and dip them in panko bread crumbs. Lightly fry the patties and then place them in the oven, and you have lobster cakes.

X Make your own panko bread crumbs. Start with good ciabatta or a similar bread. Grind the bread in a food processor, scatter the crumbs on a cookie sheet, and place it in the oven at 350° C (650° F) for about 8 minutes, but don't let it brown. Then freeze.

X Grow a few herbs in a windowsill or in your garden. When you chop up some parsley or coriander, remove the stems and freeze. They add a lot of flavour to a stockpot or a soup.

X Pesto can be made in advance with leftover herbs and frozen in an ice-cube tray. You can do the same with oil and basil.

WHEN THE LIGHTS GO OUT

Marla Allison and my stepson Brad Batten live in a fairly isolated area and know how serious things can get when there's a power outage. She says:

We are in a unique situation here in the country. Since we have a gas stove and an airtight wood-burning cast iron stove, we are never at a loss for cooking or heating sources. A couple of years ago we did lose power for three days, and I got the neighbours to join resources and cook here together. The first night we took freezers full of chicken and burgers, barbecued it all, and had a big feast. Over the next couple of days, I was able to prepare some hot foods and take them around to everyone. We always have some canned soups handy, as well as canned salmon and tuna, and a backup case of bottled water. And after the first year here, when I tried to break up coffee beans with a rock, I learned to always keep a can of ground coffee.

As for frugal living, I try not to throw anything out. I scrape vegetable peels into a bag, which I keep in the freezer, and with or without chicken bones, when there's enough, I make a broth and refreeze it. Any vegetables that need to be used get thrown into a big soup and frozen in individual servings. I'm lucky to have a juicer for all questionable-looking fruit, which can then be frozen. And stale bread becomes bread crumbs.

It amazes me when people complain about how expensive organic produce is, then load their shopping carts with meat. Eating vegetarian one or two nights a week will save a lot of money in the long run.

✕ Keep a jar filled with half paprika, half oil. Shake it up and dribble it into sauces.

✕ When you zest a lemon, freeze the juice; when you juice a lemon, freeze the zest. Lemon zest is wonderful in so many dishes and is particularly great in pancakes.

✕ Save all bones from all meats and freeze for a stock.

✕ Egg whites can be frozen and added to dishes later. Ditto for egg yolks.

✕ Overripe fruit can be cooked off and frozen. You can also use overripe fruit to make a sauce or coulis (blend with sugar and strain).

✕ Grind stale cake in a food processor. The crumbs can be used in other desserts or sprinkled on ice cream.

✕ If you shred too much cheese, freeze it. Never buy pre-shredded cheese because it's incredibly expensive.

✕ A little piece of meat can be used for quesadillas.

✕ Reuse tinfoil and disposable containers (rinse out carefully).

✕ Save liquid after cooking all vegetables. Place the liquid in a jar in the fridge and use as stock.

✕ Purchase prepared organic meals from a local shop, divide into small portions, and freeze. Just add vegetables.

✕ Add leftover vegetables to soups.

Cookbook author Lucy Waverman says: "I can't tell you how many people throw out leftovers. It takes a few minutes of creativity and essentially no work to turn them into a meal worth eating. Leftover salads make great soups with the addition of some stock and maybe a spoonful of cream. Leftover steak or roast beef makes a perfect Thai beef salad for dinner the next night. Leftover chicken can be coarsely ground in the food processor with curry seasonings, celery, red onion, and cucumber. It tastes like heaven wrapped in a naan. Leftover salmon stars in a salmon niçoise salad."

There have been times in my own life when I just stored and then tossed out leftovers. But meeting people like these foodies turned my head right around. First of all, it's wasteful not to use up everything. But even more important, these meals can be unbelievably good. It's a great way to experiment in the kitchen and let your imagination run wild.

A FEW FRUGAL RECIPES

Everybody loves to share recipes. The people we talked to would whip out little slips of paper or a file folder stuffed with ideas. Here are a few favourites from our frugal foodies.

No-Knead Bread

Filmmaker Gail Singer says this bread changed her life: "I was dazzled by this bread the first time I tasted it. It put to shame almost every loaf I have ever purchased. It is frighteningly easy, and, despite complex physical and chemical properties, allows for interesting and infinite variation. Don't buy that breadmaker. Invite some friends over. Bake beautiful bread."

3 cups of unbleached (or all-purpose) white flour
1 5/8 cup room-temperature water
1 1/2 tsp ordinary salt
1/4 tsp instant yeast powder/granules
1 cast iron pot, about 8- to 12-cup size (high-temperature ceramic or glass also works, but not quite as well)

Stir the salt and yeast into the flour. Add the water and mix gently by hand until blended: you will have a raggedy bundle of dough, more or less holding together.

Set the dough in a bowl, cover with plastic wrap, and leave in a warm-ish (say, 20° C or 68° F) place for at least 12 hours and up to 18 hours.

Drop the dough on a floured surface, and with floured hands twist the dough around gently, folding it over on itself like a hanky 5 or 6 times.

Set back in bowl, and cover for another 1 to 2 hours.

Turn on the oven to 250° C (500° F). Place a cast iron pot and its lid in the oven, until temperature is reached. (No oil, no spray.)

Drop the dough into the hot pot, place in oven, cover, and bake for 30 minutes. At the 30-minute mark, remove the lid and let the crust brown for about 15 more minutes. Pay attention the first couple of times, because every oven is slightly different.

A VERY FRUGAL FOODIE

My friend Valerie Murray is one of the most stylish people I know. Here are her thoughts on frugality and food.

I have been looking at my own behaviour and realize that I have been strongly influenced by my mother — I've been frugal for a long time, and learned every trick from her before I left home as a student.

I now understand that it is because of my mother that I feel guilty about throwing away a ham bone or a chicken carcass without making a stock. I always buy rice, dried beans, and lentils in bulk, and make a weekly soup all winter. Tabbouleh, polenta, and couscous are other favourites on rotation in our kitchen and make great leftovers. I can eat the same thing a few days in a row, but I often freeze what we don't eat for another day as my husband is not as enamoured of leftovers as I am. They deserve a second look in another ten days or so.

As children, we never ate store-bought cookies, so of course I craved them. But now I never have store-bought treats in the house. There are very good bakeries in my neighbourhood, so I will pick up a pretty cake for company if I have had a busy week. I have been to a big-box store only once, but admit that I ask friends who do go regularly to pick up large jars of Dijon mustard or bulk packages of dried wild mushrooms when they are available.

The dregs of wine bottles never go down the drain. Even mediocre wine adds flavour to many sauces. I use lots of herbs, homegrown as the seasons allow, to add freshness to food. The one thing I splurge on is great cheese. And of course good bread, as my waistline shows.

When it's ready, take the bread out of the oven and let it cool for at least an hour.

Now, think of what you can throw into the next loaf: olives, rosemary, Parmesan, sage, hot peppers, raisins, blue cheese, nuts, cumin, garlic. This bread will change your life!

Talin Vartanian's Biscuits Using Leftover Egg Whites

¾ cup finely chopped pecans

¾ cup brown sugar

2 egg whites, unbeaten

Preheat oven to 175° C (350° F). Mix all the ingredients; it should still be wet to the touch. Line a cookie sheet with parchment paper. Using a spoon, dollop the mix on the tray (you may be able to get up to 24 on a tray). Bake in oven for 20 minutes. Let the biscuits cool on a wire rack and enjoy!

Refrigerator Soup

In my youthful naiveté, I thought I'd invented Refrigerator Soup. I'd throw everything in the fridge into a big pot, add water, slowly simmer the liquid for a few hours, then drain. What you're left with is a great stock that can be used for soups. Heels of wine, cheese ends, everything went into the stockpot.

To make a soup, I added debreceni (Hungarian smoked pork sausage), fresh carrots, celery, and potatoes. It was a favourite.

Well, so much for hubris: everyone, it seems, has a version of this soup that goes back to their youth. Here's another frugal-foodie version:

Take absolutely everything in the fridge: all the sad vegetables, ends of cheese, the last bit of stuff in a jar (unless the flavours are incompatible, such as curry or barbecue sauce), and any bits of left-overs, and put them to one side.

Then attack the freezer. That last bit of pasta sauce you couldn't bear to throw out goes into the pot, the single sausage, the hot dog, the ends of dried-out vegetables in the bottom of packages that were never discarded.

Fill the pot with water or chicken stock if you have any. Add a large chopped onion and about five cloves of garlic. If I have chicken feet, they go in as well.

The whole mess is simmered in a covered pot for hours. Then drain and discard all the big lumps. What's left behind is a wonderful stock.

To make a great soup with your stock, chop up another large onion, this time very finely, along with a couple of garlic cloves. Add a cup of chickpeas or some other delicious bean you've soaked overnight (or a can of the same). Then chop up and add the decent vegetables: several stalks of celery, half a green or red pepper or both, two leeks, plus a small can of tomatoes. This concoction will cook up perfectly in an hour or so.

Non-vegetarians can add some turkey debreceni, sausage, or chopped-up ham. This unbelievably good soup can also be used as the basis of a stew or a meal of beans and rice.

ENTERTAINING MADE EASY

My friend Juliet embodies the richly frugal life. She lives alone, has a great network of friends who adore her, and in her seventies she looks now pretty much as she did in her fifties. Here's how she entertains.

Every year I give two parties, both lunches. One in the summer for fifteen to twenty-five people, and another in the winter for twelve to fifteen friends who are always generous in helping with salads and various desserts. I usually serve a couple of entrées of the simpler grain or pasta kind, along with a few bottles of wine, and hope everyone enjoys themselves (and they do, I can attest to that). Other than that, I rarely entertain except for having groups of six to eight friends over for a winter tea of crumpets and Christmas cake or for drinks in the summer garden. It's important always to keep things simple and to enjoy yourself.

Frugal-foodie mantra: nothing should ever go to waste; always cook everything twice. Learn to love leftovers.

ENTERTAINING AT HOME

For years we have celebrated birthdays with our friends Bob and Geraldine. At first we gave gifts and went to the newest, trendiest restaurants. Then we stopped giving gifts (we've all got too much stuff anyway), and searched for quiet restaurants. Since quiet restaurants no longer exist in our city, we go to each other's homes and make a bang-up special dinner. We've got a glorious dining room designed to feel like you are in the garden, though it is situated safely inside the house. The beauty of the scenery really does spoil you for most restaurants.

But one doesn't want to say: um, we can't actually afford to go out. One wants entertaining at home to be special. And sometimes an occasion does present itself. One time, after a trip to France and Italy, I brought home several bottles of olive oil and invited people over to have a tasting. The first time I did this, my friends thought I was nuts. Eat olive oil? Well, when they tasted the crusty Italian bread dipped in truly great oil, they had a different perspective. I now collect olive oil just for this purpose.

Entertaining is expensive. We always appreciate being invited out to dinner but know that the time, effort, and cost can be daunting. So offering to bring something is not an idle bit of politeness. I like it when guests bring a *specialité de cuisine* — something that's easy to make, inexpensive, and a snap to cart around (roast suckling pig, for example, is not a good idea).

My theory about entertaining is that if you have one lovely thing to eat, masses of candles, enough wine, and great company, you can't help having a spectacular time. Entertaining doesn't have to smack of expense or days spent slaving in the kitchen. Something as simple as offering lots of starters is as much fun as a complicated three-course meal. The most important thing is atmosphere: comfortable chairs or pillows, a place to put a plate (we're beyond standing up and eating), and the right lighting. You need very little else. Except good company.

Celebration with Potlucks

Potluck dinners have been an honourable way of entertaining all my life, from the church-basement suppers of my youth, to the BYOB student parties, to the way we entertain now. We have a street potluck every year, and it's always a huge success. It comprises a little competitive cooking, some really imaginative dishes, and lots of whipped cream. The host divides up the alphabet: A to J each bring enough mains to serve six people; K to Z bring enough dessert for six people. And wine, plenty of it, is supplied by the street ecology group. There are two big buckets for garbage (one for the green bin, one for recycling). And since this is an environmental group you can bet this part is observed meticulously.

Jack and I have tried taking pots of chili (untouched) and tabbouleh (not finished). But what people really love is any form of chicken or a variation on gourmet pizza. Desserts mucky with whipped cream are hugely popular. All in all, it's a wonderful party, which we all look forward to. Here are a few ideas for your next potluck:

X   If you decide to bring a salad, take it in parts. The fantastic lettuce in one bag, the bits and bobs in another, the dressing premixed and brought in a bottle. If it looks as if there'll be no takers, you can donate the leftovers to the house. Bring your own bowl and salad servers.

✗ The nibblies: take all the bits of cheese in the fridge, grate and mix together, add a little mayo and yogurt. Put the mixture on super-crispy baguette slices rubbed with garlic. Warm up to combine the flavours. Tastes wonderful. Throw in a few artichoke hearts for a change.

✗ You can't go wrong with hummus and pita bread, along with good olives. Dress up store-bought hummus by adding lemon juice, chopped-up parsley, and a big dollop of really good olive oil.

✗ Dessert: there are now really good desserts that can be bought at the supermarket if you can't figure out what to make yourself. I do a tart lemon-yogurt over fruit that tastes terrific with ice cream.

✗ Don't expect to bring food home. Package it so it can be left behind and easily stored.

The potlucks I've been to have turned into many a riotous occasion. One year, several ladies at the Toronto Botanical Garden bid on a tour of my garden. Well, they showed up with buckets of chilled wine, cheeses galore, and one of the members had gone fishing and smoked her own salmon. I took them on a two-hour tour of the garden, and we spent a good deal longer enjoying each other's company over food and drink. Now, that's what I call a winning situation.

Wine Rules

Konrad Ejbich is a wine writer, and he's also married to Talin Vartanian (Citizen Talin). There's no such thing as leftover wine in Talin and Konrad's home — any heels are simmered up with chicken stock and frozen for the next soup. They always have two or three bottles open at a time.

Here are some of Konrad's wine tips:

X We're all confused by offering wine as a present. Gift at the level you can afford. On average that would be in the $12 to $18 range, unless you are going out with a famous wine imbiber. If you can't do expensive, find something fascinating, say, a Château Moussart from Lebanon.

X If you don't finish a bottle of wine, close it up and store it in the fridge. Take the red out of the fridge and pour a glass, then start cooking dinner. When you've finished cooking, your glass of wine will be ready to drink. White can go straight from the fridge to the table.

X Don't believe that the more you spend the better wine you get. Fuzion has a brilliant wine, and it's affordable. People expect cheap wines to taste bad, so they pay more money for a wine they've heard about. But the more expensive wine may not, in fact, be as good.

X The next time you're at the liquor store buying your favourite wine, purchase the bottle next to it. Open the two together, and see which you like better.

✕ Go for the signature grapes of a country: California: Zinfandel; Chile: Carbinere (ancient Bordeaux); Argentina: Malbec; Uruguay: Pannat; New Zealand: white sauvignon blanc.

Canadian wines are labelled VQA (Vintners Quality Alliance) to signify the wines comes from the region where the grapes are grown.

THRIFTY WINE LIST

Here is Konrad's partial list of good-value wines (prices may vary, depending on your local outlet).

Good Value Reds for Under $10

Argentina
Familia Zuccardi, FuZion $7.45
Trapiche, Astica Merlot-Malbec $7.45
Argento, Cabernet Sauvignon $9.85
Argento, Malbec $9.85

Chile
Cono Sur, Merlot $9.95

France
Vignerons Catalans, Rafale Merlot $8.85

Greece
Kourtakis, Vin de Crete $8.95

Italy
Farnese, Montepulciano d'Abruzzo $7.55

Farnese, Sangiovese d'Aunia $7.55
Bosco, Montepulciano d'Abruzzo $8.00
Casal Thaulero, Merlot/Cabernet Sauvignon $7.15
Casal Thaulero, Sangiovese $7.15

Portugal
Aliança, Bairrada Reserva Sangalhos $8.50
Aliança, Foral Reserva $8.50
Aliança, Terra Boa Tinto $7.95
Charamba $9.45
Fonseca, Periquita $9.45
Sogrape, Mateus Signature $8.95
Sogrape, Dao Grao Vasco $7.95
Sogrape, Vila Regia $8.95

Spain

Candidato Oro $7.95

Castillo de Monseran, Garnacha $8.95

USA

Barefoot Cellars, Cabernet Sauvignon
$9.95

Barefoot Cellars, Merlot $9.95

Barefoot Cellars, Shiraz $9.95

Decent Whites Under $10

Argentina

Astica, Sauvignon Blanc-Semillon $7.45

Argento, Pinot Grigio $9.95

Australia

J. J. McWilliams, Chardonnay, $9.95

Hardys, "Stamp Series" Riesling/
Gewürztraminer, $9.95

Lindemans Bin 65 Chardonnay $9.95

Lindemans Cawarra Semillon/
Chardonnay $9.95

Banrock Station, Unwooded
Chardonnay $9.95

Chile

Cono Sur, Viognier $9.95

Santa Carolina, Sauvignon Blanc $8.50

Vina Tarapaca, Sauvignon Blanc $9.15

South Africa

KVW Chenin Blanc $7.95

Spain

Castillo de Monseran Viura $8.95

Rene Barbier Classic White $9.20

Konrad's Top 10 Ontario Wines

All of these wines should be consumed
immediately.

Reds

Château des Charmes 2007 Gamy Noir
"Droit" $16.95

Colio Estates Cabernet-Merlot $11.95

Inniskillin Pinot Noir Reserve $18.45

Southbrook Vineyards Cabernet-Merlot-
Shiraz $14.95

Trius Cabernet Franc $15.25

Whites

Creekside Estates Sauvignon Blanc
$13.95

Konzelmann Pinot Blanc $10.95

Pelee Island Pinot Grigio $11.95

Peninsula Ridge INOX Chardonnay
$12.95

Strewn Semi-Dry Riesling $11.95

COOKING FOR A CROWD

If you're hosting a wedding or a shower, or any other major celebration, then you may choose to cook for the crowd instead of paying for a catered affair, which could cost at least $100 per person for a three-course meal. Cooking for a crowd can be daunting, but if you rustle up a group of friends you can also have fun making a special occasion even better. The most important thing is to be organized, know your budget, have a menu firmed up, and shop sensibly. Think about those amazing people who feed the hungry, and let them be your guide for a frugal banquet.

Writer Stevie Cameron is one of the most inspiring people I've ever met. She lives the frugal life, though she barely notices it, she savours everything so deeply. A Paris-trained cook, Stevie applies the same principles she uses at home to the church soup kitchen where she's been volunteering for seventeen years. They can feed up to 250 people at a time at St. Andrew's, and they have become famous for their meals.

"The thrift part is that we're willing to take the trouble to make good food," says Stevie. "We have enough volunteers who love to cook. We even have a potato group (the Glebe peelers) who sit and peel potatoes (100 lbs), carrots (10 bags), apples (a case), and have a good old gossip."

The principles they use are very much the same she learned at the Cordon Bleu in Paris when she was young: "We basically use

French cooking techniques: we build the flavours by sweating all the vegetables (carrots, onions, and celery) in oil or butter, depending on the cook."

And though they don't depend on donations, they might get, say, a box of chicken legs, which won't feed 250 people, but can be used for a chicken pot pie or a soup. "We cook fabulous food and we don't waste anything," Stevie says. "When we received a case of mangoes, Michael Smith, Chef at Large, was doing a documentary on us. He said, 'You can make a crumble out of anything.' So we made a Mango Crisp, which none of us had had before.

"We never use prepared foods except for instant mashed potatoes (as thickener for chicken pot pie) and Robin Hood pie crust mix."

Stevie has the same attitude toward food at home as she does at the church. She doesn't buy prepackaged food, with the exception of the pie crust mix, and she makes other kinds of crusts from scratch. "I buy locally, where I can, and I buy organic meat. It's expensive but I use much less. I always eat seasonally. I drive to Niagara in the fall and make all my own jams."

Building flavours doesn't have anything to do with being cheap: even wilted vegetables can go into a CrockPot and turn into something wonderful. But it's taking inspiration from all sources and being observant that makes the true frugal foodie.

Our relationship to food is always complicated. And it's so tied up with how you were raised and the kind of food you ate as a kid. The frugal kitchen may take a lot more planning and chopping, but when you haven't got much you are more likely to be careful of how you use what's available to you. Good food, well prepared is one of the most loving things you can do for yourself, your family, and your friends.

CHAPTER 4

THE FRUGAL
HOME

I came from a frugal home though none of us knew it at the time. Home's home to a kid. My mother, who was left alone with three kids through most of World War II, cut corners in order to live on a military salary in downtown Winnipeg. She ran a sparkling house and fought loneliness by listening to the radio, a habit that's lasted a lifetime for me. I can get more mending, fussy cleaning, and (very occasionally) ironing done while listening to a decent program — the reason why public radio was invented.

We kids learned how to dust, do laundry, make a bed with hospital corners (that skill actually came from Guides and Scouts), and help with the cooking. We buffed floors to high shine by sailing around on the hardwood with big old socks on. There was no question of leaving a light on in an empty room. It just wasn't done. You removed your shoes so that you wouldn't track dirt — or worse — into the house.

It was a disciplined generation. And that discipline stood many of us in good stead when we grew up and later owned our own homes. Even so, I'm not sure if everyone felt as overwhelmed and inadequate to the job as I did. Obviously my mother, as a fourteen-year-old immigrant who made her way alone into this country, had experienced way more privation than I could imagine; but my father, one of eight kids in a contractor's household, grew up knowing how to do everything: plumbing, carpentry, small renovations.

They passed on a lot of their skills to us kids. But when I first got married, I realized I wasn't quite as smart as I thought, and, like most people, learned how to run a house on the job.

HOW TO BUY A HOUSE

Buying a house is a notoriously complex issue. I grew up in a generation that dictated you had made no progress in your life unless you *owned* your own home. Rent was considered throwing good money after bad. So we were house-poor for years until the mortgage was paid off.

I bought my first house with my second husband, Jack, in 1967. The kitchen ceiling fell in the day the deal closed. "Good," said the architect, "we don't have to tear it down."

We were renovation pioneers on our street. Friends thought we were insane, buying on a street heavy with rooming houses. Forty years later, this area is now lusted after by the trendy and well-to-do. But we bought it because the house could be changed drastically, had a backyard, and the kids could walk to a really good school. There was a great little theatre up the street, a church that held superb concerts, and many ethnic stores all along the main drag.

What we didn't know would have filled an encyclopedia. We didn't know you could run out of money and have no windows; that even though school had started, the work wasn't finished and that we'd still be shovelling plaster dust out of the beds for months. But our story was the norm, something we weren't aware of at the time. We've renovated many times since and never want to leave our house because it's exactly how we want it. They will have to drag us out of here toes up.

We were lucky because we bought at a good time. We also looked at about thirty houses before this one spoke to us. I often pass some of the others and think how different our lives would have been. Serendipity sometimes speaks out loud, and this old house has shaped our lives. When you buy a house, you have to work out all your priorities, not the least of which is the longevity of your stay. It's not much fun to think about the end when you are just beginning, but it's worthwhile asking yourself these questions before investing in a new home:

- How long will we live in this house?
- Are we willing to move in a couple of years?

MR. FIX-IT

Ted Johnston is a whiz at buying old, neglected houses and fixing them. After renovating twenty properties in as many years, he's now become a professional agent. He offers this invaluable advice for those who are thinking of buying a fixer-upper.

I look for a twist, something unique about the house. Location is not enough for me. Something about the house has to stand out or have the potential for me to create something that *will* stand out. I have never had a home inspection done, and I rarely make an offer with conditions. A cash offer and quick close saves money, and you get the place you want but cheaper. So do your homework before you go hunting. Then, before making an offer, consider the following:

- Know what you can afford and get financed (the banks like 25 percent down).
- Know what you can and cannot handle in terms of renovations and repairs.
- If you aren't handy, then get a home inspection done (about $300), which provides a capital plan so you can strategize how and when you will make the necessary repairs.
- Avoid any home with foundation problems unless you know for a fact the lot it sits on will make it worthwhile.
- If there are water issues, move along.
- Location is huge. The more places you can walk or bike to, the more you will save on gas. If you are looking for a cottage, buy on the side that will get you out of the city fastest.

- Take advantage of every program the government has going on home ownership. It may be a lot of paperwork but well worth it when you get a rebate. Then you can buy that expensive dining-room set you didn't think you could afford.
- When selling a house, curb appeal is important. Buy a house that has none and then create it — picket fences are a sure winner and a garden big or small at the front is gold.
- Buy dirty and sell super clean.
- Keep it simple. Give definition to every room and the outdoor space. Your own elbow grease will save you more money than you can imagine.

I recycle and reuse everything. I spend money on things that are important, such as a good toilet or a stunning light fixture, and save on things like doors or tiles, which are easier to recycle or find in junk stores. When I go to garage sales, I look for construction materials — anything I can reuse for building or renovating. I have a huge door collection so that when I'm renovating a house, I can create custom doors and cupboards. Always check out the remaindered bins or as-is bins. Visit reuse-it centres for sinks, doors, windows, and even trim. These shops will save you lots of money. Overall, use your time wisely and try to do most of the work yourself. See if friends are willing to lend a hand.

- Should we buy a fixer-upper, knowing we can resell for more money in a few years?
- What should be fixed first if a complete renovation isn't possible?
- What will happen when the kids leave home?
- Is this the house that will see us out?

The problem of what you can and cannot afford, of course, is central to the whole house-buying project. Being honest about the kind of mortgage you can afford to carry, let alone getting into renovations, is tricky. Though I've lived only in this one house, I've done enough renovating to know that a budget is usually as ephemeral as the proverbial line in the sand.

RENOVATING AND MAINTAINING A THRIFTY HOUSE

Even if you can carry the mortgage and all the costs of a house, major repairs are what can actually break your spirit. A couple of years ago we had to unload a huge amount of money into a new roof. We knew this was coming, and saving up for a big renovation you can't see is discouraging. But save up you must. I have a separate house account and dab a few bucks into it on a regular basis for just such events.

The old saw "If it ain't broke, don't fix it" doesn't work for home ownership. The basics are to never, ever let a tap drip and change washers regularly or get someone in to look at them. Dripping taps and toilets mean wasted water. Make sure that the drainage on your property is moving away from the house, and if it's not know that you'll have to do something about it at some point. This might include new grading and parging where the walls meet the soil, adding sump pumps or French drains — all very expensive. Wiring, unless it's up to code, will always be a drag on the household account if it's ignored.

Always do as much as you can yourself. There are a multitude of do-it-yourself (DIY) web sites that give you some of the basics while you wait for a pro to show up and, who knows, maybe you'll uncover a hitherto unknown aptitude. But unless you are absolutely confident that you can complete one of these tasks well, you might have to call in an expert.

If you do outsource the work, hire the best professionals you can find. If they aren't top-notch, it will cost you down the road. I know from bitter experience. The term "craftsmanship" should be familiar to the people who work on your job. *Caveat emptor* is fundamental to renovating. If you work with really good people, it makes a tough job a pleasure.

Being content with less and putting money into boring things to keep your home running smoothly are all part of maintaining a frugal household.

Heat

Heating a home can be incredibly costly, especially in a persistently cold climate. Precious warmth can escape through cracks in the floors, ceiling, doors, and windows. There are a number of ways to plug these pesky leaks, and at very little cost. First, get out a candle and see where little puffs of air are getting in. Or hire a specialist who will conduct a heat audit of your house. They tell you where all the leaks are and how to fix them.

In winter my friend Juliet hangs fleece curtains made from blankets on all the doors and windows in her lovely old home. She buys the material at discount stores, and they are an ideal way to cut drafts. If you choose the right fabrics, they look cheerful and are easy to wash. "In a pinch they can be taken down and put to their original use — wrapping the body of a chilly guest," says Juliet.

You can also buy or make draft evaders, and duct tape is great around leaky windows. Consider the following suggestions as well:

- Buy high-quality thermal windows (make sure they have good gas fills or they will be useless).
- Install good storm doors. There's a style that has a screen you roll up in summer, and has a storm window for winter.
- Insulate everywhere, especially floors. You can lose a lot of heat through them if you have a cold basement.
- Double up on rugs (a cheap one below, a more attractive one on top). It's a great look and will help insulate frigid floors.
- When you aren't using a room, keep the doors closed.
- Use ceiling fans to keep warm air from hugging the ceiling.
- Close the vents in rooms you aren't using to concentrate the heat in living areas, and reduce how often the furnace clicks on.
- Wrap heating ducts to hold in the heat. But tell the hardware

clerk what you are doing to make sure you get the right kind of wrap and tape.

- If you have radiators, deflect heat from walls by using heavy aluminum foil screens behind them.
- If you aren't using the fireplace, plug the openings. Otherwise, heat rises right out of the house.
- Replace furnace filters every couple of months.
- Buy small electric heaters, turn off the furnace, and use them to heat an occupied room (but make sure to keep the kids away from them). They are terrifically efficient because they can be switched off as soon as the room is warm enough.
- Keep your thermostat down at night to 15° C (60° F), and don't turn it much above 20° C (68° F) during the day. Wear a sweater.

It would surprise most of us to know how leaky our houses are. But there are lots of DIY solutions you can try to help conserve on heating bills. Just don't ignore problems.

Electricity

Electricity is another household necessity that can cost you more than it ought to. It may seem obvious to switch off all your appliances before going to bed at night, but it's important to unplug them as well (okay, not the fridge or freezer). Electricity is leaking through those plugs at all times and you're paying for it. Never leave home for any length of time without unplugging all unnecessary appliances and electronic devices.

There is a theory that if everyone unplugged all of those machines with the little red lights when they aren't using them, there would be enough energy to air-condition North America. This may be an urban myth, but the point is that unplugging even small items can bring your electricity bill way down. Here are a few other ways to save on electricity:

- If you have a natural gas hot water heater, wrap it with insulation, being careful not to get near the pilot light; ditto the pipes. This approach will keep the water hot for a longer period of time. If you don't know how to do this yourself, get someone competent to do it for you or you could end up with a dripping mess.

- Lower the temperature on an electric hot water heater from 65.6° C (150° F) to 55° C (130° F), but make sure your dishwasher runs efficiently at this temperature.

- You don't need the clock on the stove, the microwave, or the home entertainment unit. Wear a watch and learn how to switch these functions off. Use them only when you have to use a timer.

- Use a battery-powered wall clock instead of a plug-in.

- Turn off the oven and the stove before you need to. They hold heat and food will continue to cook. This includes the electric kettle.

- Switch off automatic thermostats. Do it by hand, and you'll use up far less fuel.

- Pull out plugs during electrical storms, and disconnect the lines from the telephone to the computer. An electrical hit can wipe out a computer.
- Pull your fridge a few inches away from the wall so it uses electricity more efficiently.
- Turn off the dishwasher dryer cycle and let dishes air-dry.
- Set dryers and dishwashers to run late at night when electricity is the least expensive.
- Put lamps on dimmer switches, and use the newer form of fluorescent lights.
- Learn to read your own meter.

Electricity is one of the greatest of all modern living essentials, and we take it utterly for granted — until it fails. It's wise to know as much about it as possible so we use it efficiently and responsibly.

Water

Water is the essence of life itself and yet we squander it in the most astounding ways. In the future, water will not always be as readily available or as cheap as it is now. So here are a few suggestions that will help you use less of this dwindling commodity and save you money:

- Make sure you are on a water meter so you can track how much you are using. Find out how to read it by going to your water company's web site.

- Replace a big old water heater with a new on-demand hot water tank. They are expensive, but they make so much sense. You heat up only what's needed at any given moment. But make sure you get it installed properly.
- Take quick showers and not baths. Or give up a shower for a day or two just to have one lovely long soak.
- Buy a big rain showerhead. They are soothing and disperse the water in such a way that the cost is worth it.
- Buy an eco-friendly showerhead that restricts the flow of water to a certain gallon or litre.
- Never run a dishwasher until it is filled. Pick "light" wash and stick to it.
- Buy an energy-efficient dishwasher.
- Keep a jug of drinking water in the fridge so you aren't running the tap waiting for the water to chill.
- Fix leaky faucets and toilets immediately. More water is wasted this way than probably in any other manner and can lead to damage to walls and tiles. It may cost a little more getting a professional in, but think of the long-term savings.
- Take a container in the shower with you, and use the water you gather for your houseplants.

You can also save money by learning to do small plumbing chores yourself. For instance, snakes aren't expensive, and if you went in with a couple of neighbours (especially one with lots of storage space), you could buy one between you and learn how to use it properly. It could save a lot on plumbing bills. And it's not impossible to learn how to change a washer; all you need is a wrench and a little elbow grease.

Air Conditioning

It's horrible to wander about outside and hear the drone of air conditioners fill the soft summer air. They fling masses of pollutants into the atmosphere. But few of us want to lie in bed dripping with sweat during a heat wave. So both for the savings and the environment, you might want to think about using an A/C carefully and efficiently. Here are some ideas:

- Don't let the air conditioner run when you aren't in the house.
- Raise the temperature at which the A/C kicks in. You can save up to 5 percent on your electricity bill.
- When you're running your air conditioner, close any vents in rooms that aren't being used (you can seal them with duct tape), and make sure all the doors and windows are closed.
- Utilize the furnace fan system, which takes cool air from the basement and moves it throughout the house.
- Install ceiling fans in the rooms you use most often to disperse cool air in the summer and warm air in the winter.
- Consider investing in ductless A/Cs on each floor. The upfront costs are high, but it's way more efficient than central air because you cool only the areas of the house you are using.

- Plant huge trees around the house; they are the best air conditioners possible. A mature deciduous tree with a large canopy will lower the temperature of a nearby building up to 10° C (50° F).
- Use awnings and shades effectively. In my parents' day, the first person up in the morning closed all the windows left open at night, drew the shades, and we had our summer gloom and cool.
- Cut the power off the central air conditioner during the winter; the heating element could use up electricity all winter long. Put the power back on twenty-four hours before using it.

If you decide on using window A/C units, make sure they fit properly, seal them tightly, and store them at the end of the season after cleaning. I regret installing central air conditioning in our house. We seldom use it and it doesn't reach the third floor. If I were to do it over again, I'd have ductless A/C units on the first and third floors only, and use them judiciously.

THRIFTY SHOPPING FOR THE FRUGAL HOME

What was most interesting about what defined the best bargains for our frugal home owners is that emotional investment was the main prerequisite. If the cost of the item was within reason, financially speaking, if it was something they really longed for or loved, that in and of itself made it a bargain.

DOWNTOWN PIONEERS

For the past twenty years I've been dazzled and inspired by the neighbours in the other half of our semi-detached house. We can hear each other living, though not quite breathing, through the walls. I knew they were different as soon as they moved in — they installed a clothesline in a neighbourhood that was busily getting rid of them to show its upward mobility.

Laurie Matheson and her husband, actor R. H. Thompson (Robert to us), run the archetypal modern frugal home. When they bought the house in 1980, they became downtown pioneers and decided to reinvent city life. It began because as Robert says: "Actors can't afford to own a house unless they can figure out how to do things themselves. You don't hire a plumber, you do it yourself."

Since there's no such thing as unemployment insurance, medical, dental, or pension plans provided by the workplace for artists, they have always been good at saving. "We started out being frugal because we didn't make much money, still don't," says Laurie. "But most of our frugality now stems from environmental concerns."

Their philosophy is that if you are thrifty in small things, you'll find money for the bigger things you want and need. It's about spending smart on a small scale, saving as you go along, and buying smart on the big stuff. Laurie didn't even bother with a credit card until she was well into her thirties, had two little kids, and didn't want to carry wads of cash while travelling.

Robert and Laurie are the ones who can rescue everyone on the street when the electricity goes off on the coldest winter days. They have wood-burning stoves and a thermal fireplace. Robert's reasoning about wood stoves is as much about saving money as the environment: "Dead wood stores carbon. When wood rots, the carbon is returned to the atmosphere, I'm neither adding nor subtracting from the carbon cycle. The wood must burn clean enough to keep it within this natural cycle, and with our kitchen's wood stove we get an intense short-term heat. We've also built a thick brick screen behind it to absorb enough heat when the fire goes out and keep the house warm almost all night. And bubbling away on top of the stove is a humidifier. It's essentially a pot of water with a hole in the lid — it's very old and very efficient.

"When we turn on the furnace we add to our carbon footprint; when we fly we do the same. But when we turn on these wood-burning fires, we're carbon neutral." Robert zips around collecting unpainted construction pallets (usually made of old-growth pine), which, left for garbage, would head to a landfill. They are densely grained and will take years to degrade. By collecting and burning them, he saves taxpayers the cost of sending a truck to Michigan.

The Big Splurge: a Tulikivi thermal mass fireplace, which graces their living room. It cost $8,000 plus installation. They had to increase the support in the basement and install special vents so the heat reaches the rest of the house. But it gets the most heat from the least amount of wood. It has almost eliminated the need for using the furnace, except for a few desperate weeks in mid-winter.

Water is Robert's other passion: hot water is one of the biggest gobblers of energy when there's a tank at one end of the house and a tap at the other. So he installed a small tank under the sink that gives them hot water on demand. They have a hot water tank close to the washer, dryer, and shower (all located in the main bathroom).

This project evolved into the Solar Hose Episode. Robert noticed hot spots on the roof (rotting shingles being baked by the sun). He bought two 50-foot lengths of black hose, coiled it on the roof, then ran the hoses into the bathroom through a window. One hose was attached to the sink, the other to the shower. He'd run the water into the hoses and let it sit until the water heated up. "On hot summer days you couldn't put your hand in it," he says. It did look a little odd to this neighbour, but through the experiment their hot water bills for two summers amounted to only $120.

Laurie has always loved the clothesline, but the dryer has become a sticking point over the years. She uses it only during the winter when it's vented so the warm air is drawn back inside. Robert would like to have a drying closet. At the moment, she says, that means draping damp laundry over the banisters, which she has definitely nixed.

They are now constructing Styrofoam winter shutters for those days when the temperature hits -20° C (-4° F). Robert collects old pieces of Styrofoam, and Laurie looks for attractive fabric ends to cover them. They pop them into the window to keep the heat in, and they have a painterly look, given Laurie's creative eye.

Robert's dream is to have a fridge that would switch off automatically when the temperature drops outside and cold air can be piped into the fridge. At the moment they cool things outside in winter, never open the fridge if they don't have to, and bake cookies in an oven cooling from the casserole. In the meantime Robert is still tinkering with how to get hot water into the bathroom when the sun doesn't shine.

When we asked people what household items they would never skimp on, couches and mattresses were at the top of the list. Both are considered splurge-worthy, and both must have quality and comfort. Some worried that buying second-hand upholstered furniture was risky because of the resurgence of bed bugs. These little devils can live for years before making their presence known, and then it's a battle to get rid of them — one that costs in time and money and many a sleepless night.

Our frugal home owners do a lot of research. They know the price range of the items they are interested in purchasing, and are prepared to walk away if it is too expensive. But one of the most interesting pieces of advice was to shop alone. *You've* done the research, *you've* got a list, and you *don't* want to be swayed by someone else's opinion, however kindly intended.

On the other hand, swapping items with friends and family was high on the priority list. Anyone who is downsizing is happy to get rid of stuff, especially if you offer to pick it up. Networks such as freecycle.org post masses of free stuff, and terrific second-hand shops offer quality goods as well. As Margaret Atwood says: "It is circulation that keeps the blood running, the economy too." So when you shop for appliances you are not only doing yourself some good, you are helping out the economy.

Shopping for Appliances

The first rule of thumb when shopping for major appliances is to measure the space you've got to make sure you are getting the right size machine. Second, ask for a demonstration (I didn't when I bought my last dishwasher, and now I hate it because it's noisy and clunky). Finally, when you receive your appliance, look for nicks, damage, and soil marks on the item before using it. You may need to make an exchange.

Citizen Talin has done hours of research on large household purchases. Here is her advice on two.

Citizen Talin on Buying a Mattress

Talin Vartanian was recently sent on assignment to investigate the mattress industry. She unearthed a collusion between the manufacturers and the retailers: "Manufacturers will make a mattress that is virtually the same on the inside with slightly different stitching on the fabric. They will sell the mattress under four different names to different retailers.

"So here's what happens. If you want to price compare and do it over the phone, you ask for your favourite mattress by name and they'll say they don't carry it but have a similar one in stock. So it's impossible to know the exact price. It's trickery because it doesn't allow for comparison shopping and it's done intentionally. This goes on with many products, so rigorous investigation is always best."

Here are Talins's tips on how to get a good deal on a mattress (and it's advice that extends to all purchases — big or small):

1. Always do your homework. Hit the phone to price compare. Read blogs and consumer complaint sites to get a sense of what the service is like when something goes wrong and what people think of the products they have.
2. Ask friends about their particular product. What make is it? How long have they had it for? Has anything gone wrong with it? Would you buy that model again?
3. Speak to someone who knows. If you are looking to buy a new appliance, talk to your appliance repair person.

4. Go to the manufacturer when you can. They don't sell direct to the consumer, but they will walk you around the showroom and talk you through the products. Ask for a list of all the stores that sell the product and write it down.

5. Find friends who want to buy as well. Even if the product you're asking for is shipped to three locations, you can ask for the best price on three.

6. Don't be nasty or cruel when haggling or negotiating on a price. Just ask: "Is that your best price?" You'd be surprised at the additional discounts many retailers are willing to offer.

7. Research all the lingo so you are talking their language. Create a glossary for yourself.

8. Read the fine print. Retailers and manufacturers will often try to weasel out of a warranty. If there is even a tiny stain on a mattress, for instance, the warranty is completely nullified.

I wish I had been as well armed when I went out on my last mattress shop. I bought a very expensive one, influenced by the company's vast advertising campaign. Nowhere do they mention that the material releases off-gasses (chemicals). It stinks. If I had done my research, I would have learned about off-gassing. When I wrote to the company in despair about the skunky smell, they said it would last for only three months and I would have to do all sorts of elaborate things to get the stench out beforehand. But that important bit of information is left out of the advertising, and the company I bought the mattress from never mentioned the issue either. When I called the seller to complain, it was as though I was the only customer to have ever had the experience. Research, research, research.

Citizen Talin on Buying a Dishwasher
Here are the main issues to think about before purchasing a dishwasher:

1. Of paramount importance is the way a dishwasher stacks. Take a good long look at the racks and see how adaptable they are. Do they allow space for extra large platters, pots, and baking pans?
2. Noise level is another issue. Except for the very high-end machines that cost thousands of dollars, every dishwasher will make some sound. Ask for a demonstration to make sure you can live with it.
3. Length of washing time. Most people set their machine for a "normal" wash, which takes the maximum time. A "light" wash, which takes about twenty to thirty minutes less time, can sometimes do an adequate job. Experiment with it.
4. My repair person, Mr. Suzuki, says if you find a machine with a dial, buy it; they are better than the computerized brands. The number of options on most machines are unnecessary because most people use the "normal" setting all the time (see #3 above).

All major appliances, according to my large-appliance repair guy, Steve Brannan, are not nearly as well made as they used to be unless you get into the insanely priced high-end products. So keeping an older appliance going is probably the first route to follow. Get yourself a good service repair person. And this does not mean signing a service contract, which is how retailers and manufacturers make a lot of money. Service contracts are strictly another way to part you from your hard-earned dough.

Frugal Home Furnishing

Putting together the frugal home with style takes a little concentration, but it doesn't have to take a lot of money if you've got a bit of flair. Back when we had few resources, I painted our dining room top to bottom in black, restored the hardwood floor, and lit a lot of candles. The results were pretty dramatic. I furnished the room with an old round oak table I found in a junk store and the sideboard, which I bought for $20, is still with us and looking even better today.

Janice Lindsay is one of my heroines. In her role as colour consultant (see Notes on page 195 for her terrific book), she changed my life. Jack lives upstairs in his apartment, and I live downstairs in mine. I was in a state of despair about my rather shabby half of the house. In came Janice who spent an hour with me looking at paint chips. It seemed expensive at the time, but I realize now that when you are up against technical problems anywhere in your house, your garden, or your wardrobe, hire an expert. In the long run Janice saved me money by helping me make decisions (I knew what I wanted but not how to get there) and give the house a fresh new start, vibrant with colour. I have been unbelievably happy with it ever since.

I asked her for her best shopping tips, and here's what she suggests:

- Don't throw good money after bad. If you don't like something, don't build around it. Either wait until you can redo the room, or as you move forward go in a direction you like even if it doesn't match. The bad will look worse and eventually you will deal with it.

- If you like something — for example, a funky, mismatched, old-fashioned kitchen — keep it.

- Function is more important than aesthetics, but chances are the things that work do not seem unattractive.

- Don't ever give anyone a present that they have to live with — i.e., an object they can't eat, drink, or burn — unless you are absolutely certain that they desire it and are willing to take on the burden of ownership.

- Workmanship is at the heart of thrift. Quality antiques are much better buys than badly made new. Good new is like acquiring a piece of art: it requires a trained eye and it's expensive, but it will be worth it if you love it.

What makes an aesthete such as Janice Lindsay happy are these kinds of splurges: fresh flowers, candles, art, nice bedsheets, a good knife, down cushions, and music. "A change can be stimulating and energizing, and it can purge stale energy or unwanted association," she says. "It can be used as therapy that lasts."

Next, I wanted to remake my basement bedroom. I looked for expert help, and designers Lindsey and Gerry Anacleto came into my life. I have never had to buy anything else for this room. It is so beautifully sculpted, and, best of all, I can't mess up the design. This feels to me like the ideal of the frugal life: making things complete, a quelling of desire for acquisition. It's all here around me.

Here are Lindsey and Gerry's expert home shopping tips:

- HomeSense is a chain that sells furnishings at huge discounts to support many community projects. They offer great items at great value.
- Check out garages sales and second-hand furniture stores — off the beaten track. Do some research or you'll be shopping where everyone else is looking for the same thing.
- Used office furniture stores have great deals for the house.
- People throw out some beautiful pieces if you aren't too proud to take them from the side of the road.
- Go to warehouse sales offered by well-known furniture manufacturers or showrooms.
- Sign up for a mailing list for showrooms or manufacturers you like.

Lindsey and Gerry don't make a habit of haggling, but would certainly consider doing so if a piece of furniture has been sitting around a showroom for a while. They always inquire about sales, and will ask for a discount even if the sale is over. When they buy floor models, they always ask for a reduced price. "What I usually ask," says Lindsey, "is when their next shipment is coming in, and then I offer to buy the one on the floor. When you shop at a store on a regular basis, they are more likely to know you and you can get away with asking. I have also found that if the staff knows a mutual friend or you have some kind of connection, they are more willing to wheel and deal."

Auctions and Estate Sales

Writer Stevie Cameron has been a collector since she was a kid. She cannot resist going to auctions looking for bargains. Almost everything in her house is a find (from estate sales, auctions, bargain shops). When she was looking for a good down sofa, she prowled ads for estate sales. She knows a place that will replace the down and re-cover furniture for a reasonable price. And chances are she might already have a bolt of cloth picked up at another auction that will do just the trick. She will even buy old quilts and have them refluffed. "I don't think I've ever bought a new piece of furniture except for appliances and good technology for work."

Here are Stevie's tips on buying at auctions and estate sales:

1. Find an outlet where you can get to know the people and who will talk to you even if you aren't unloading major amounts of money.

2. Go to the preview, then go back again. You'll fall in love with everything the first time, and the second time you will automatically wonder, "What was I thinking?"

3. Go early, get a decent seat, prowl through the catalogue.

4. You will probably lose the things you love the most (everyone else will want them too).

5. Talk to someone on the floor and ask, "Is there a lot of interest in this item?" If even one other person is interested, he or she is probably going to buy it.

6. Buy because you know something about the piece.

7. Be sure to check for cracks and chips. If something is chipped the value will go down. So buy like you buy art: only if you love it, not as an investment.

8. Look for small finds: get a couple of cups and saucers or some silver forks if you can't afford to buy a set.

Stevie recommends taking a course on how to look after good furniture, china, glassware, and silver, and to look for artisans who know how to mend glass, lace, and beautiful artifacts. They still exist; finding them just requires going through networks or maybe even looking them up in the Yellow Pages.

Lawn, Garage, and Street Sales

For decades I have been trolling our neighbourhood streets on the days before garbage pickup. I learned about finding treasures on the street from a young actor Jack interviewed in New York City back in the 1960s. This chap had furnished his whole apartment with junk from the garbage, and it looked pretty hip, jazzy, or far-out (whatever term was in vogue at the time). Once I was alerted to this form of scrounging, it amazed me what people would get rid of.

Looking around at leftovers requires a keen eye. You can be trained but it takes time. Here are a few tips:

1. If it's leaning, leave it alone. Chances are you can't fix it either.
2. Don't be deterred by a scratched-up finish. Sandpaper and a good paint job will cover up a multitude of sins.
3. Check out books on antiques from the library so you'll recognize a treasure should it come across your path. Learn to distinguish copies from the real McCoy
4. Have a look at eBay for what's collectible right now.
5. Grab stuff the minute you see it, even if it's not quite right and you have to put it out again yourself. It won't be there in twenty minutes.

One of our greatest trash-to-treasure finds occurred when a neighbour tossed two great wicker chairs. They needed only a little repair and a good paint job, and we used them on our front porch for fifteen years. When I was sick of them, I put them outside with a big sign saying FREE. Gone almost instantly, on to yet another life.

GARAGE SALE JUNKIE

In the home of novelist Edward O. Phillips, I spotted one of the most stunning pieces of cobalt-blue Arabia in my pattern (Valencia). "Got it at a lawn sale," he crowed. No amount of money could entice him to sell it to me. Phillips wrote a very funny novel about lawn sales called No Early Birds, *which I read before setting out every year. So we had to ask him for the last word on garage, yard, and lawn sales.*

First, dump the preconceptions. Arrive with an open mind. Disappointment dogs those who hope to find the top for a Wedgwood gravy boat (fine china having been promised in the classified ad) or that size-6 Chanel suit (vintage clothes having been listed as a lure). Try to imagine yourself as Adam or Eve facing the Garden of Eden, and every step brought discovery. It may be highly unlikely that you were looking for a Venus de Milo with a clock in her belly, but when confronted with such an object who could refuse? A bead curtain made from cowry shells from the Caribbean may not have been high on the "must find" list, but when seen in all its tawdry glory, furthermore for only a few dollars, who could walk away empty-handed? Here are a few tips for the garage-sale neophytes looking to take the plunge:

- Bring your own shopping bags. Do not expect them to be supplied by the vendor.
- Be well supplied with change and small bills. Don't waste time niggling over nickels and dimes. While you are haggling over 15 cents, someone else has snapped up the Waterford decanter the owner believed to be merely pressed glass.
- Beware of sales where nothing is priced, unless you are good at bargaining.
- Do not appear too stylish or well groomed. Clean but mended is a useful look: hair

- pulled back and fastened with a rubber band; no expensive *Sex and the City* handbags; poor but not too proud, neither craven nor cocksure. Timex is preferable to Rolex.

♦ A studied neutrality is excellent camouflage, especially when you realize that the piece of tarnished plate is actually sterling.

♦ Diffidence is useful. You may lust after that little upholstered chair, but behave as if you might, just might, find a place for it.

♦ Beware of price tags. A platter may have the $5 price tag pasted carefully over the large chip on the rim.

♦ Be sure to check out each plate in a stack; the chipped and heat-crackled ones often end up on the bottom.

♦ Go late in the day for big-ticket items. Vendors holding sales do not want to carry heavy furniture back inside. In addition, an hour or so before closing time there are bargains to be had.

♦ If business is slow and you see something you really want, chat up the vendor. Buy a couple of small items, then appear to spot the Lalique vase thought to be carnival glass. What is the price for the lot? Often the blanket cost will come in under the individual prices totalled up.

♦ "No Early Birds" is a garage-sale mantra, more observed in the breach than in the practice.

♦ Nowadays dealers are on the prowl: they will try to get the one good piece by buying up several items as camouflage.

♦ Beware of appliances: gleaming kettles, pristine blenders, and funky toasters. These items come with a murky past and a questionable future. Innocent of warranties, they may or may not play havoc with your circuit breakers. Better to buy a new appliance from a large discount chain.

One last bit of advice: solidly middle-class neighbourhoods, those with row houses and duplexes, offer the best bargains. The high-end postal codes offer merchandise that would be refused by the Salvation Army: old curtain rods, back issues of *Esquire*, plastic flowerpots with dead bulbs still intact, worn flip-flops, and a nest of tables badly in need of refinishing.

Sadly, there is a golden age for most activities. Think of theatre during the reign of Queen Elizabeth I, the novel during that of Queen Victoria, American musical theatre from the 1930s to the 1960s, or the vitality of television during its formative years. There was a true golden age for garage sales, namely, the middle decades of the twentieth century. Baby boomers were retiring and scaling down. The garage sale still had the charm of novelty, before turning into a cottage industry.

Today there is an aura of rank hucksterism: the private sale has become big business. One can even hire people to organize the sale "*trésors cachés*," which usually means garage sale items at antique-store prices. But with diligence, backed up with high-hearted optimism, one can still find sales that hark back to the golden age.

One final word: not to be overlooked as a source of serendipitous surprises are the annual church bazaars, usually held around Christmas and Easter. Treasures are to be found, as people will proffer up good pieces "for the church" instead of squirrelling them away for yet-unborn grandchildren. The atmosphere of a church bazaar is welcoming; one usually runs into friends and enjoys those three-minute catch-ups, somewhere between better jewellery and attic treasures. Good baking is to be found in abundance, which is useful for those who donated the marble rolling pin to last year's sale.

And yet, and yet: what could possibly be better than the anticipatory thrill of setting out on a beautiful May morning, well armed with bags, change, and hope. Out there the ultimate, still-undiscovered object awaits. And No Early Birds be damned!

Best Home-Furnishing Bargains

Some of my most enchanted evenings with friends have been spent knocking back wine and swapping stories about foraging — from cheese to paint to shoes. It's like watching veterans swapping war stories. We frugal home shoppers are proud of getting the right bargain for the right space or purpose and for the right price. And everyone has an outrageous, top-of-the-list Great Find story. Like talking about plants, the discussion can be charmingly competitive. But the following define a fantastic bargain:

Years ago I saw an old black cabinet in a junk-shop window for $7. I brought it home, cleaned it up, and it turned out to be a beautiful piece of early-Canadian fruitwood now estimated to be worth more than $2000. — *Photographer John Howarth*

I took two dressers from the side of the road, then painted them into a masterpiece. — *Contributor Rebecca Grim*

I went into a big second-hand furniture depot when they happened to be at the point of receiving items. The owners were very receptive to my offers, as furniture had not been unloaded from the truck and therefore unnecessary for operators to find space for it on the floor. — *DIYer Sheila Delaney*

I wanted a funky-but-functional bedroom light fixture to replace the standard-issue square one. I looked at a lot of so-so options that ran at $100 and up before I finally found the perfect one in the children's department at IKEA for $30. — *Business Systems Analyst Katherine Hajer*

I was looking for a cheap set of bookshelves while attending school and poked around a government-surplus store. To my surprise, I ended up finding a $70 antique corner cabinet, which was somewhat rough around the edges. I knew it was made of good-quality wood (not chipboard) and looked like a piece I'd keep for a very long time. — *DIYer Alix Davidson*

My bargain of a lifetime was from a clipping my mother sent about an auction in a small town. I sat there all day with my eye on a mahogany tallboy. I got it for $150 and it was Georgian, worth a fortune. It's still perfect. On another out-of-town sale I found a hundred pieces of pottery, a lot of which were cracked. But some were Quimper, which I collect, and I got them fixed. — *Author Stevie Cameron*

My best bargain was finding a junk store out in the country with a cache of cobalt-blue Depression glass stuck way in the back of the shop. I have dreams about that place. I bought as much as I could afford. I started collecting this wonderful work, and still use these pieces every day with pleasure.

MY BEST BARGAIN   By Colour Consultant Janice Lindsay

I bought a huge walnut Victorian sideboard "from a castle in Belfast," if you believe what the labels say. I could not afford it. I coveted it for a long time and then it was sold. I pined and pined and mentioned it every time I went into the antique store, which I did frequently because I was a stylist at the time. Then I got a call from the dealer: "Look, we have that sideboard you loved so much in storage, and the guy who put the deposit down never came back. So we are selling it at half price, cash only. Someone else came in and measured it to see if it will fit his place, but we don't want you coming in for another who-knows-how-long asking about it, so we are just letting you know."

Yes, it was very expensive, but it was worth way more than I paid and it is worth even more now. I have had the good fortune of enjoying it every day. Thrift is about trying to buy less by buying well. Then you never get tired of things because they transcend fashion and style, and are a part of you because they serve you well.

Home Evolution: Decorating on a Shoestring Budget

We were told time and again that evolution, not revolution, is the best way to deal with redecorating. Moving furniture around was an excellent example of how to change your space without your wallet's involvement. It's about doing a little at a time, all the time. Katherine Hajer's mantra is: Repurpose, Reuse, Recycle.

Repurpose: I have a great set of tealight holders that were

originally crocus-bulb vases. The crocus bulbs went mouldy,
but it fits a tealight perfectly.

🏠 Reuse: About a third of my furniture once belonged to some
relative or another who moved and couldn't fit it in their new
place. Old furniture of mine has met the same fate.

🏠 Recycle: Paint, podge, and varnish can work wonders.
My printer stand is a 1960s fake wood-grain end table
that has been covered with black rust paint to match the
rest of my furniture. My old coffee table was a bargain-
priced IKEA table topped with a collage of Ansel Adams
photos from an old calendar, and coated with Varathane
to make it stainproof.

The Anacletos are adamant that all the possessions we accumulate
today clutter our houses, our minds, and makes us crave change — ergo,
needing more stuff. By ridding your life of old tchotchkes, cleaning,
painting, and changing the hardware, a dramatic evolution can occur.
They recommend sorting out what you have to have and what you are
willing to budge on right at the beginning of a project.

Here are some of the Anacletoses thrifty decorating suggestions:

🏠 Get as much sunlight into the house as possible. Get rid of
any heavy drapery that blocks light.

🏠 Paint, paint, paint!!! Painting has the most dramatic impact
on a room and is the cheapest way to change a space.

- Hanging pictures is a great way to freshen up your home. You will fall in love with your house all over again.
- When tiling, choose a field tile that is inexpensive for the main wall, and then choose a more expensive accent tile as a border.
- Replace hardware on older furniture or cabinetry, and you will have a completely new look.
- Refinish hardwood instead of installing new floors.
- Paint old wood handrails to give them a fresh look.
- Paint a tired-looking staircase and install a carpet runner.
- Replace a countertop in a kitchen and paint.
- Get a new front door — it always changes how you feel when you come home.
- Always have fresh flowers on display; a beautiful bouquet on a clean surface can make you feel so much better and allow you to endure your space a bit longer.

Our other frugal home owners had these suggestions for decorating on a shoestring budget:

- Maintain your furniture and carpeting with regular steam cleaning and Scotchgarding.
- Purchase the best-quality fabric (on sale) and reupholster a vintage chair or loveseat; add gorgeous toss cushions and a throw.

- Beautiful doors and detailed moulding will transform a room.
- Install a mirror on the ceiling to make a low entrance feel like a palace.
- Mirrors can make a small hall look larger; fewer possessions can make a small apartment seem much roomier.
- Buy mistinted paint, which works out to be a fraction of the price and you can come across some interesting colours.
- Buy art. Art lasts a lifetime, and gives your home a feeling of individuality.

The constant evolution of a home is a fascinating way to look at your personal history. I remember feeling completely rejuvenated when I replaced the 1970s light fixtures and installed more contemporary ones. It changes the whole look of my kitchen. With the addition of a lot of mirrors, the darkness of the first floor brightened up immeasurably.

I must say I like to look around my house on a regular basis to see how it can be refreshed. It's not about doing a major decorating job, it's about perking up a space you already love with what you have in a way that will transform the whole house. And that's what we're all trying to do: small, affordable transformations that will bring much joy.

CLEANING THE FRUGAL HOME

My husband is a tidy person. He believes in the L. Rush Hills aphorism "Tidying as you go is half the fun." Not me. I'm a messy person and cleaning my own house is a tussle. I'm allergic to perfume and just

LOVE WHAT YOU BUY By Fashion Writer Karen von Hahn

Real bargains are items that turn out to be genius forever, regardless of how much or how little I paid. In that respect, an old Chinese restaurant sign that I found at an Asian importer was probably my best find because I've enjoyed it everywhere we've lived and I still get a kick out of it every day. When I came across it, I wasn't looking for a fabulous artifact and didn't have a lot of money to toss around. I called my husband at work to tell him about it. Of course, he was in the middle of something and couldn't really understand why I was so excited to spend $250 we didn't have on an object like an old Chinese restaurant sign. I ignored his advice and bought it anyway, and haven't regretted it since.

I know this to be true: not everything has to be brand new and purpose bought. Don't pass up anything you love if it's under a certain price point that, in the grand scheme of things, you can live with. You will regret it forever. But don't ever buy anything unless you really, really love it.

about all industrial chemicals, so I *have* to use alternatives. And they are affordable. Cleaning house is one of the least glamorous aspects of home ownership, but there are ways of doing it that can have health benefits and save you money.

The Cleaning Basics

The basics for all frugal cleaning are the ones my friend Juliet Mannock has followed for many years. She's the type of person you call when you're completely befuddled by a project. Here's how she uses the basics:

- Buy baking soda at a bulk store and divide it into three uses: baking, cleaning, and medical use.
- Buy steel wool and divide it into the painting and cleaning departments.
- Buy bleach, dilute it at once, transfer it to a large juice container, and use it for crafts or for cleaning.
- Buy white vinegar and divide it into crafts and cleaning containers.

There are lots of web sites about how to use the big four (baking soda, vinegar, borax, and water). My friend Esther has used these products to clean the house for years. Here are her tips on using the big four as well as some gathered from web sites:

Baking Soda

- Buy baking soda in bulk and save on expensive packaging.
- Use it in the fridge to get rid of odours, then recycle it by using it as a cleaning agent.
- A paste of baking soda and vinegar can be effective on really bad bathtub rings, shower tiles, and shower curtains.
- Rub on surfaces to remove scuff marks.
- Clean the sink drain with a mixture of 1/2 cup baking soda, 1 cup vinegar, and 1 cup water.
- Sprinkle on a smelly mattress when you are changing sheets.

(This is actually how I finally got rid of the awful smell from my mattress.)

Borax

- Add half a cup of borax to the wash cycle to cut grease in really dirty laundry.
- Use as a deodorizer by sprinkling it on mattresses and couches (this will discourage bugs as well).
- To remove stains, dampen the stain with water, sprinkle on borax, let dry, and vacuum.
- Use borax to scour pots and pans without leaving a scratch.
- Mix 1 teaspoon of dishwashing soap and 1 teaspoon of borax in a litre or quart of warm water, and spray outdoor furniture and tiles to avoid mildew.

White Vinegar

- Spray your window with water and vinegar, and wipe clean with newspaper for a bright shine.
- Add a cup of vinegar to the washing cycle to get rid of mildew and other foul odours. Then wash normally.
- Ammonia may cut grease, but it's also dangerous. Use a spray bottle filled with four parts water, one part white vinegar instead.

Vinegar has its own great web site, www.vinegartips.com, which I found to be one of the best cleaning guides on the Web.

Laundry

Margaret Atwood is particularly galled by our attitude toward laundry. "No one knows how to do laundry anymore," she says. "All the things we were taught are the best basics: wash whites separately and dark colours together." She is confident that coloured sheets will make a comeback because they don't get dirty as quickly as white ones. "We went into white so they'd look like those nice German hotels. And I predict retailers will sell replacement elastics for fitted sheets. They'll be on sale by every cash register." Here are some of her other thrifty laundry tips:

- Shift sheets the old-fashioned way. There were no fitted sheets back in the day, so when Monday rolled around, you'd take the bottom sheet off to wash it. The top sheet became the bottom sheet and then you put on a new top sheet. It's half the amount of washing.
- If you've got old king or queen bedsheets, cut them vertically down the middle, hem them, and you've got single sheets.
- Load the dryer up and preset it to run during the night when electricity is much cheaper.
- Only get the machine going when you have a full load of laundry, and use the proper setting. Don't do more than you have to.

- Get a drying rack or a retractable clothesline and hang-dry clothing three-quarters of the way through, then put them in the dryer. You keep the warm, moist air in the house instead of paying money to blow it out.
- Iron while clothing is damp and they'll keep the press. It makes more sense than drying and later spraying them with water.
- Try the home dry cleaning kits if you can stand the chemicals. They aren't nearly as bad as the chemicals used by dry cleaners.
- Learn how to take out spots. Dripped wax can be taken out effectively if you stick it in the freezer, and pick off the lumps. Then, using a paper towel under and over the wax, apply a hot iron and it will melt out.
- Leave clothes out in the sun if they need bleaching. The sun is the best stain remover there is.
- Use a drying rack and a clothesline.

Atwood is convinced that outdoor clotheslines will make a huge comeback. "Everybody in Europe has a laundry rack. We lived in Madrid, and you took laundry up to the roof and it would dry in a couple hours," Atwood says.

What I find weird is that I can live like a European when I'm in Europe (line-dry laundry), but the minute I get back home I revert to the dryer. But I'm trying to be a little more sensible about it. I now dry thick and fluffy things together, light lingerie gets a few minutes and then finishes drying on towel racks. My next purchase will be a foldable drying line.

🏠

A friend once told me: "If you rid any room of one-third of the stuff, it will look 100 percent better." She was right. I felt like I was surrounded by babbling in my living room. So when I took out all the family photographs and put them where I can see them all the time (my bedroom), removed most of the tchotchkes people had given me, edited the books to just a few special ones, and cleared every single surface, it was like taking a deep breath. My Zen moment had arrived.

One of my heroines of taste is Valerie Murray, and her words keep banging around in my head: "The things that I surround myself with are often less than perfect, but I seek quality materials and design. They are not 'faux' in texture or history. If I had more money I probably wouldn't buy perfect even if I could. I don't need the biggest or the newest. I want comfort and quality in materials and good design. If an object was designed well in the first place I will not tire of it."

I'm convinced that though this is a frugal house, it has a sense of comfort and style that is just right for someone like me: a writer, a gardener, an unfussy sort of person. It won't be photographed by interior-decorating magazines because it's way too eccentric. But then that's not always a bad thing. Comfort is the main element in my life. It's very thrifty.

CHAPTER 5

THE THRIFTY
GARDENER

What started out as an innocuous though frugal move decades ago, turned into a complete career shift. I'd been a freelance magazine writer for years, and decided that if I was going to change the garden, it would have to pay for itself. I wrote a story about my garden renovation for a glossy magazine — the fee ($400) became that year's garden budget. My utter joy in writing about gardens soon outstripped my interest in interviewing people. Plants held all the essence and mystery of life. And soon enough I was making a living as a bona fide garden writer.

I did go into instant tithing mode, however, returning a percentage of what I'd earned to the very place that was now making me a lively and comfortable living. But then, I'd always had a garden budget. Anyone who tries to do anything in the garden without a budget is crazy. There are way too many temptations: tools, rocks, pools, and plants, plants, plants.

My friend Karen York's vision of the ultimate thrifty gardener is one who spends the day outdoors, wearing fifteen-year-old pants and a discarded denim shirt, carefully transplanting seedlings into a bed enriched with decomposed apple cores and veggie peelings from the last year, and watering plants with rainwater from the various buckets and tin drums sitting about for just that reason.

When she's being serious, both of us are as close as you can get to classic frugal gardeners. But any ideas of thrift go right down the tubes when we go out on what always turns into competitive plant-hunting trips. Gardening can be as inexpensive as you want it to be. Just be careful of who you shop with.

PLANNING A GARDEN

One does learn lessons every minute spent in either a nursery or a garden or with a hortbuddy. Here are my own hard-and-fast rules on planning a garden:

- 🌱 Lesson #1: Always have an annual budget. Observe it.
- 🌱 Lesson #2: When making a garden for the first or even the

fifteenth time, have a vision of what it is you want. Make a plan, however simple. Hire an expert, but make sure you have a sense of what you want so they have guidelines to follow.

🌳 Lesson #3: Read the tag. If it says Zone 7, and you don't live in Zone 7, this plant might be fine for one year but will struggle ever onward until it gives up. You can probably create a Z7 microclimate in your garden if you live in Z6.

🌳 Lesson #4: You can't have one of everything. I used to grab anything rare and unusual because I had to be the first, the one to experiment with the unusual plants. It's folly and you end up losing plants and money.

🌳 Lesson #5: Get rid of as much grass as you can. Grass is a very nice feature but a small one in the scheme of things. It adds little to the ecology of where you live and gives almost nothing to the birds and insects who depend on our gardens for sustenance.

The thrifty gardener is automatically going to be an observant gardener. By following these rules, I guarantee you will save buckets of money. You won't be buying plants that will head invariably to the compost heap, and you will have a vision that makes sense for the kind of life you live.

Be as patient as possible and take a long view of gardening projects, planning to work on it over a number of years instead of aiming for a slam-dunk instant transformation. If you can afford it, consult a professional.

In the end you'll save money. They know how to cut costs, are able to give you a plan that can be installed in stages, and can show you how to overcome technical problems. But don't accept a plan or design that is just twelve of this and a dozen of that. Sameness in a garden is boring.

Alas, so many landscapers, even professional designers, know nothing about how plants grow. Many have a repertoire of a few dozen plants, and they will plant and replant them from garden to garden. I am also a plant consultant, and when people are unhappy about their gardens it's often because a landscaper has put in fifteen of the same thing — when the fad of planting in blocks is not done well, it's not aesthetic and half the plants will eventually need to be removed. Unless Piet Oudolph, the great Dutch garden designer, is doing this kind of installation, it usually means the designer hasn't a clue about how the plants grow and what their cultural needs are (light, soil, and space, especially space). So make sure you check out what they've done before. If it's not your style, take a pass.

Here are a few things to think about while you're in the planning stages of your garden:

- 🌳 If you do get professional help, spend time examining what the designer has suggested and make sure it fits in with your own needs. Discuss things if you aren't sure what's what.
- 🌳 Don't overplant. This is the oldest garden design trick in the book: lots of plants, instant results, and once you've paid the bill half of them will be crowded out or die.

🌳 The frugal gardener is a mindful gardener. If you have a computer use it for research; if not, hit the libraries and bookstores. It's way cheaper than rejigging a whole garden because it's not what you had in mind.

Have a look at my book *How to Make a Garden* for good basics (see www.marjorieharris.com).

STARTING A GARDEN

Don't take gardening so casually that you forget the fundamentals: know your land, your soil, your light, and your budget. Designing a garden can be as simple as one perfectly placed tree and a lovely seating area. But it's important to have a focal point, whether it's a shrub or a grand sculpture. I have an obelisk smothered in clematis ('Duchess of Albany'), and you can see it through a screen of other plants, so it leads the eye into the distance.

I found out years ago that gardening in pockets works best. Take one small part of the garden (maybe the focal area) and concentrate on it. Then keep moving away from the house as you understand plants and add to your repertoire. You'll find you've established a palette, and will have had time to form a style for the garden. You can't rush this process.

Before you venture into the garden to do the real work, be sure to stick your hands in the soil and learn about its texture and density. Check out how many hours of sunlight hit different parts of the garden each day. Figure out where the water will come from. And take what you've got before you into account. In other words, the first step is to think things through.

Our thrifty gardeners love to get their fingers in the dirt. Here are a few of their personal suggestions:

- Try as much as possible to limit the garden to what you can do yourself, whether it's plant production or maintenance. Being a thrifty gardener means being a realistic gardener.
- Think ahead, take the time to plan, and that way you won't buy all sort of things you won't like or need in a few months' time.
- Plant a perennial in a pot as a focal point, then plant it back in the ground in the fall.
- Grow drought-resistant plants native to your area.
- Drought-tolerant plants often have grey or furry leaves, and can survive really dry weather, as will prairie species such as purple coneflower (*Echinaceae* spp).
- Only grow plants that favour your area, soil conditions, and climate.
- Use your own compost to half fill pots before adding potting soil, but keep potted plants to a minimum. They demand a lot of watering and weeding, and often die off suddenly. But contrariwise always have lots of annuals around to fill sudden gaps.

- Make and use compost tea as your fertilizer — very sparingly as too much can produce massive foliage production and few flowers.
- Plants that are somewhat stressed bloom much more enthusiastically . . . stress is good in this department.
- Use more perennials, flowering trees, and shrubs with varying bloom times. This minimizes using annuals and means lower expenditures. Once the garden is in place, plant new varieties.
- Plant as many trees and shrubs as possible if you want to cut back on maintenance and work. Masses of annuals take a huge amount of time and effort (and a young back) to keep all that deadheading going.
- Use more grasses and larger plants like *Rodgersia*, *Ligularia*, *Aruncus*, *Anemone*, and *Echinacea* — whatever spreads and fills the garden with colour.
- Grow plants from seed — it takes time but saves money.
- Trees will inevitably grow and sunny areas will become shady. Take this into account when you are planning.
- Try to make as many parts of your garden as low maintenance as possible, relying on plants that for the most part take care of themselves.
- Keep a small shovel and pots in the trunk of the car so you can take pieces of plants from friends' gardens whenever you visit — with their permission, of course.

- 🌳 When shopping with fellow gardeners, buy one of the expensive varieties and then eventually start clones for each other.
- 🌳 Buy later in the season to take advantage of sales.
- 🌳 Pick one area of your garden each year to update and "refresh."
- 🌳 Over-winter favourites indoors from year to year.
- 🌳 Plant bulbs from those gifts of potted plants from friends.
- 🌳 Check web sites that advertise free garden tools and accessories.
- 🌳 Chip twigs and branches, and use the bark as paths. It saves you from having to purchase gravel . . . and it looks good.

"Right plant, right place" is an old adage that is essential to the thrifty garden. But you must have a vision. What will make you happy in your garden? What reasonable ideas do you have? What should it look like in five years? The latter is really important. Don't be fooled: you can't make an instant garden unless you have tons of money. Even then it wouldn't be very satisfying. But you can have a really good garden over a few years. It's not needs versus wants here: you must be aware of both your needs for the garden and what you want — your vision of what the garden should look like in several years. Can't have one without the other.

Buying Plants

I always tell people to make a list before they go to a nursery. If you are as much of a plantoholic as I am, it's a disaster not to. Everything looks fantastic. I end up with a porch full of plants and have no space for them. Don't overbuy. There will always be more plants. But if you see something special, something you can't live without, get it immediately because it won't be there later on if it's that good.

One of the most important rules in buying plants is not to go for the biggest one you can find. A small, well-grown plant might look unimpressive at first, but it will stand a much better chance of acclimatizing to your garden in the long run. It will also probably be cheaper. The frugal gardener has patience, if not a large pocketbook.

Don't be intimidated by the need to BUY NOW that happens in garden centres all over the country around the May 24 weekend. The good nurseries bring in new plants regularly; so much so that now late August and early September are considered a second planting season. If you've got six weeks before you know a frost is likely to hit, you can plant anything but evergreens (wait until spring to plant them).

From the very beginning, I've been a frugal gardener — with exceptions, of course, and every one of these expensive little peccadilloes involved an overweening ego. The first major splurge was buying a tree so rare that each one was numbered. *Franklinia alatamaha* was a beauty. It was smothered in camellia-like blooms that first year, and, considering the $400 price tag, I liked to show it off. I was one of only two people in a city of two million who owned the tree (the other being Karen York, who purchased it during one of our competitive shopping trips).

The second year it looked pathetic (Karen's turned into a vine support), and it continued to flag year after year. I had bought something rare and unusual all right, but stupidly ignored the fact that it was out of its climate range. I finally gave it to someone who lives in the right area, and it thrives. Rarely, after this experience, have I flung away money on such an inappropriate plant. Karen is normally a rational gardener, but even she succumbed to this foolishness. Normally she would advise the following:

- Get plants that give a lot of bang for the buck (four-season appeal, whether it's flowers, foliage, bark, form) and aren't fussy or difficult to look after.
- Have a strong underlying structure (woody plants and hard-scaping) so the garden looks good even if you don't bother adding perennials and annuals.
- Plant bulbs that will do their thing indefinitely.
- Avoid fast-growing plants such as forsythia and privet, which need constant trimming.
- Try to get plants in the right place the first time around.

All retail outfits, from supermarkets to big-box stores to your local mom-and-pop flower shop, will have end-of-season sales. I'm of two minds about this. Always ask yourself: is that plant really a bargain? Plantoholic Margot Belanger is almost impossible to restrain, but even she knows her limits: "When using the term 'bargain' and 'plant' in the same sentence, you are not likely to use the word 'cheapest.' Never has the expression 'you get what you pay for' been more apt than what you have to pay to get a healthy plant. It's always about value for dollar at the nursery. Buy plants early and liberate them from their pots, as opposed to waiting until the garden centre at your local supermarket is about to close for the season. What are the odds that plants labelled three for $10 at the beginning of the season will have much life left in them by the end of June?"

Don't even think about haggling during the regular season. Over the years, I have established relationships with several superb nurseries, and they will tell me if they feel they can sell a plant for less than the ticket price. But this is a business that works on such small margins that the idea of haggling over plants is just plain vulgar. I sure wouldn't do it. Most good nurseries have points cards, valued customer days, seniors' discounts, and sales — get in on all of the ones you qualify for.

Your relationship with the staff at the local nursery is critical. Apart from the fact that it's fun to go to a place where they know your name and your preferences, the staff at well-run nurseries will save particularly good specimens for you, or even find plants you would never have discovered yourself. And the only way you'll be able to get that kind of service is at a proper nursery. Now, this is not to say that I'm against the big guys. Their prices are often incredibly low, so take advantage of them. But, personally, I like to talk to someone who knows the plants and loves what they are doing.

From Seed

Seeds are the most tempting items in garden catalogues: all those rich colours and magnificent blooms. And you are usually looking at them in the dead of winter. The result is a tendency to over-order. You want everything. If you have limited space, get a seed buddy to share the expense. You might want to consider this idea of sharing for all your garden needs: mulch, potting soil, and expensive equipment.

I admit I'm no seed grower. But here's what rose expert Mark Disero suggests: "Thrifty gardeners coordinate and buy their seeds in the spring. If a group of three gardeners buys ten packets each, when the seedlings are ready to share, they can all have thirty cultivars (for the price of ten)."

The easiest way to do this is to be realistic. How many vegetables are you really going to have space to grow? How many containers can you accommodate? Don't waste money on seeds; they are expensive. To save money, save your seeds. And you can't save hybrid plant seeds, which is one of the big reasons why heritage vegetables are becoming so popular. They are open-pollinated, and you can collect the seeds at harvest time to replant next spring. Some plants are self-seeders. Keep them under control by pulling out all but a few (larkspur, forget-me-nots, poppies).

Seeds can be started in just about any container with a drainage hole (good way to use up margarine tubs). Cardboard egg cartons are useful and so are eggshells (poke a hole in the bottom). Set them on abandoned cookie trays and water from the bottom.

You can save seeds by keeping them in a cool, dark, dry space (the fridge is not always the best place because it might fill up too quickly). Seeds can last for many years so don't be surprised if you come across some that will do just as well this year as they did three years ago.

Vegetables

If you decide to grow your own vegetables, makes sure you have a few facts under your belt:

- Vegetables need six or more hours of sunlight a day.
- They need attention every day: watering, weeding, picking out bugs, pricked out, thinned, and, in general, a lot of TLC.
- Plant some vegetables among your perennials. One plant will help the others by drawing in beneficial bugs to help keep the garden clean and healthy. (Have a look at my book *Ecological Gardening* for a gazillion tips on this.)
- Don't plant too much or you won't be able to give away your harvest. Think of zucchini and how quickly they become inedible.
- Make sure you have someone you'll be sharing your harvest with. Deciding on who grows what can turn an individual garden into a community garden with very little organization.
- If you start in early spring, divide the seedlings based on the best light and soil conditions for each plant. Harvest can be one big helpful party.

- Always have pots of herbs and keep them as close to the kitchen door as possible.
- Reseed great stuff, such as Swiss chard and arugula.
- Mulch between rows to preserve water and keep weeds down.

Fellow frugal gardener Nicole Jodoin grows herbs in perennial borders. She says, "I like to have lots of lavender, lemon thyme, and rosemary, in particular. I make herb mixes for cooking, such as my own blend of herbs for a poissonade, which we use when cooking fish. I make herbes de Provence and bouquet garni, as well as fresh teas from lemon balm, pineapple mint, and peppermint in the summer. I always grow small tomatoes in pots on the deck or patio. This year, I planted three varieties of heritage tomatoes from seeds that I purchased at a local 'Seedy Saturday' event."

Growing a vegetable garden takes time and effort, but it does save on those grocery bills and makes for terrific gift giving.

The Lawn

A lawn is just a flowerbed that hasn't happened yet.
— Margot Belanger

A lawn is any green space that is cut short for walking.
— Uli Haverman

I'm told time and again that gardening is a major hobby in North America. According to a Garden Writers of America poll, people are concerned about the environment, so they garden. They want to recycle, so they garden (compost, mulch, return plastic containers), and they want good mental health, nutrition, and fitness, so they garden. But, of course, most of the money they spend is on the lawn.

It is a mystery to this frugal gardener why people are so interested in lawns. They are just one small part of the design of a garden, or should be. Nice negative space to a positive space, as they say in design.

I got rid of my lawn back in the 1980s when I decided it wasn't going to work well under all the trees I live among, and it took too much work for too little reward. I like to spend my time in the garden, not on top of it. Then there's the weeding and the seeding and the general messing about. Try replacing the lawn with a great product called Eco-Lawn (be careful, there are imitation products that look the same but aren't). Broadcast the seeds, and a lovely grass quickly emerges. It needs cutting only twice a year and gives a soft, shaggy carpet effect. It's a mix of hardy regional grasses and it works a treat.

Lawns are expensive. You have to water them unfailingly or they will go into dormancy during a heat wave. This use of water is not always going to be possible in the future. You can save yourself a lot of money and effort by slowly eliminating the size of your lawn. It's not doing what you want your garden to do: be a magnet for insects (though it will attract animals if there are lots of grubs underground).

Get rid of that gas mower. Electric mowers are better, and now they've gotten cheaper. Best of all is the least expensive option: a well-balanced push mower. It's way more efficient at cutting grass, and you will benefit from the exercise. If you use a mowing service, hire only those who have push mowers.

Never use a leaf blower, and don't let people in your area do so either. It takes about the same time to rake or use a straw broom to clean up leaves.

To get rid of lawn, try this trick I saw the great geranium grower Phoebe Noble do in her vast garden in British Columbia, where everything grows ridiculously fast. Take about fifteen layers of newspapers and wet them. Place the newspaper all along the edge of the grass you want to bump off. Then add a layer of straw for the winter. By spring all of this will be mostly composted down and the area free of grass. Here are some more lawn-related tips:

- Plants *not* to replace the lawn with: sweet woodruff (*Galium odoratum*); creeping Jenny (*Lysimachia nummularia*), unless it's the golden form, which doesn't move fast.
- Never, ever buy variegated goutweed (*Aegopodum podagraria* 'Variegata'). This stuff isn't called weed for nothing. It runs about 25 metres (80 feet) in every direction, and once it takes hold (anywhere from four to ten years) it will elbow out everything in its path. Variegated goutweed is best grown in a container, preferably a concrete tub, and is to be used only in dead dark shade.

🌱 Watch out for Japanese knotweed (*Fallopia japonica* syn *Polygonum cuspidatum*). It looks pleasant enough with its nice long tassels and six-foot-high stalks, but it's a noxious weed, which will kill off everything else, including trees and shrubs.

I mention these plants because it's important to see errors before you make them. These plants may look good at first, but they are sneaky. The amount of time, energy, money, and help you'll need to get rid of them is astounding. What starts out to be a nice little $3 plant will end up becoming a $300 excavation job pretty quickly.

Garden Tools and Accessories

You can go crazy buying garden tools and accessories, so here is what's essential:

🌱 A good-quality, stainless-steel garden border spade with a flat, sharp edge. You can do almost anything with it, and it's particularly great for creating a sharp edge around a bed.

🌱 A transplanting spade with a dish and long handle that makes it simple to dig up perennials. With a good one, it will be easy to lift out a shrub.

🌱 A superb trowel with a stainless-steel shaft. Mine's twenty-five years old and still works perfectly. Don't skimp.

🌱 Two pairs of secateurs: a cheap one and a tough by-pass for slightly larger stalks.

- A kid's rake. It gets between plants, and you don't want to rake too much anyway.
- An excellent hose with a brass nozzle. I'm still using the ones I bought thirty years ago.

I do buy garden gloves all the time and then forget to put them on, but they are great. A hat is always good, as well as something to kneel on. If you design the garden properly, there will be a seating area so you've always got a place to plunk down your equipment. Carrying your gardening tools around in a pail is useful, or in one of those great foldable leaf baskets or plastic trugs.

The rest is candy coating. Even so, it's impossible to look at a garden catalogue without seeing about a dozen things I can't live without. I do my best to control this urge (and so should you!).

DECORATING A GARDEN

I love having a variety of ornamentation in my own garden. I can't resist collecting stuff, displaying *objets trouvés* on fences, or just leaving the odd bit of sculpture lying under a plant as a surprise. These small decorative elements add important texture to any garden. Then there are the big things: glorious containers (preferably ones that stay outdoors all winter); obelisks for vines; and decorative screens. They can be cheap (stuff picked up by the wayside) or expensive (bought at high-end garden stores); but they should be durable. I can never understand why people will crab about the price of a gorgeous container and then go out and spend $200 on dinner. The container will last for years.

Amortize everything you buy for the garden: if the item will last for twenty years and you are looking at it every day, how much is that worth? Twenty-five cents a day would be about $1,800. A penny a day would come to $73. What is it worth to look at something with those intangible aesthetic qualities that brings pleasure all year-round, perhaps for decades? So the next time you look at the price tag of something you love, don't gag: amortize.

A word about furniture. No one willingly puts crap in their living room, but they will in the garden. Buy the best; don't buy plastic. Follow all the rules for furnishing the house. You'll have good stuff for years and years; low-quality furniture falls apart quickly, especially when it is up against the elements outside.

Hardscaping

Hardscaping is the term landscape architects use for raised beds, gazebos, stone patios, walls, and on and on. It's all the stuff that isn't softscaping (plants). It's what designers know about, it's what they do well. Depend on a professional if you need a French drain, a new deck, or massive stonework. They know scale, which is a really important consideration.

To keep hardscaping costs down, fish materials out of landfills. To beautify your garden with stone, use stone found in local construction sites.

"I have always loved low stone walls, flagstone paths, patios, and the like," says gardener Deborah McPhedran. "When hubby brought a few samples of gorgeous dolomitic limestone (golden brown with occasional blue-grey) back from a site inspection, it was fate. We'd recently destroyed our own front garden with a reno of the front vestibule, so we were looking to landscape it and the back garden, and needed to get rid of the grass altogether. All in all, we must have collected 10 to 14 tonnes of material (with the permission of the site supervisor), using dollies, a 6-tonne-capacity rental truck, and wearing steel-toed boots on our feet. Now that most of the stone has been incorporated into the garden, it's looking good. It would have been a terrible waste. Thankfully, many other people felt the same way, and were thrilled to have access to this material for repurposing their own gardens."

"You can build retaining walls in gardens with broken concrete," says Lisa McCleery, another thrifty gardener. "All you have to do is open your mouth to say that you need it, and suddenly you'll have more than you could imagine! The walls can look as interesting as you want . . . and if you don't really want them to show, just plant along the edges with small creeping sedums. After a year in the garden, the walls take on an interesting patina. I did one in my backyard, where the stone is almost completely hidden by plants; another is just down the street from me and is used as a free-standing planter; the last, and my personal favourite, is a wall built out of bricks, concrete, old drainage pipes, and broken clay pots. It's a statement about reusing. The only cost was to move the rubble there, but it sure does look fabulous!"

Furnishing a Garden

Use your imagination to furnish the garden: hang artifacts like old fireplace screens on fences. It takes only a few bucks to clean them up, and they spend an eternity looking ornamental. I placed all my original Salvation Army wooden furniture around the garden. Thirty years later I'm down to one rotting chair. I love it as much now as I did then.

A garden lends itself to this kind of nostalgia, and should be filled with as many memories as it is with plants. However, you have to group collections and use good aesthetic judgement. There are many ways you can tart up a garden for free. I've tried everything from discarded sinks to old tubs. A friend of mine even used the abandoned claw-footed bathtub the workers tossed in her backyard during a renovation. Use chairs and ladders as plant stands. Look at anything that will hold soil as a potential container. But don't be too cute about it. Those old boots should probably be put out in a yard sale.

But here's a lovely idea from rose guy Mark Disero: he found a nice old window with glass intact, painted it a gorgeous colour, and set it up so that it "frames the view" (sorry, that's a garden joke). It looks great in a field, and I've also seen it done effectively on a deck where it provided a little spot out of the wind. So be creative and be willing to adapt when furnishing your frugal garden.

Containers

I love containers, but hate dragging them in and out of the house in winter and spring. But by investing in a few large ones, I've saved myself work and money. They have a permanent place in the garden, and need only a clean-up and new soil and plants in the spring. They are big investments initially — hundreds of dollars. But when I think of all the clay pots that have exploded or fallen apart, the other pretty things that cracked and were thrown out, I don't resent the cost. I have one container I paid $250 for back in the 1980s. It seemed a fortune then, but it is still in perfect condition and I have it placed so I can see it all year-round.

Here are some things to think about before you invest in a good container:

- Buy containers that seem too large. Little ones create a ditzy effect.
- Go to garage sales and look for objects that could become interesting containers. I have found wonderful copper washtubs (add holes for drainage) that look even better with age.
- Never buy too many containers. They're fun to collect, but you may be faced with a massive storage problem.
- Look for good sales at big-box supermarkets and specialty gardening stores. When they have deals they are incredible.
- Buy containers made of metal, wood, or some type of stone, concrete, or terracotta. Don't buy plastic. Good-quality containers may be expensive up front, but with care should last you a lifetime.

THE WEDDING GARDEN   By Ted Johnston

When my partner and I decided to get married, a wedding planner told us that no matter what we said, our guests would want to give us gifts, even though we had everything we needed. "Be specific," she advised. "Tell them what you *do* want so you don't end up with a pile of silver you *don't* need."

So we asked our guests to buy us trees. They did, and we have marked each one so that when we're in the garden we have fond memories of the friends who gave them to us. An aunt held a wedding shower for us and told everyone to bring plants from their gardens. We received a huge variety and put them all in one place, which we now refer to as The Wedding Garden.

- Look for garden accessories second-hand at garage sales, thrift stores, or antique shows.
- Containers can be used as garden art, and, as such, they are priceless. It's worth investing in good quality, both for durability and for the aesthetic pleasure they bring. They are a splurge.
- If you can't resist collecting containers, place them in groups, unplanted, as a sculptural element.

One last word of advice from my gardening friend Margot: "When looking around for interesting alternatives to more conventional containers or planters, one should always ask, 'Okay, it's cheap, interesting, and amusing, but can anything actually grow in it?'"

MAINTAINING A GARDEN

Maintenance is the last thing people think about when they start a garden. It should be the first thing. How much time will you spend in the garden composting, mulching, weeding, and fertilizing? It's sensible to be realistic and work backwards. Design a garden that will accommodate the amount of time you have to spare for it. If you have only a few hours a week, then plan on getting up a little earlier to do a few garden chores; it will improve your day. I promise.

Compost and Mulch

Absolutely every one of the many frugal gardeners we talked to said to compost. It really is the magic bullet of gardening. My kids had an area of their own early on. It was sort of a concrete basketball area. When they left home, I busted it up and used the concrete to make a raised bed, but the soil was dead. Not a worm in sight.

It took a few years of piling on leaves, garden waste, and building a compost in the same area (the worms come by magic, telepathically) to transform the space formerly known as *le jardin de refusé* into what it is now: one of the most productive parts of the whole garden.

I steal everyone's leaves and don't even bother grinding them up as many of our thrifty gardeners do. I just dump them into plastic bags, bang a hole in the side, and roll them around all winter. By spring they are starting to break up. Toss them into the compost bin to finish things off.

There's not much you have to do to start a compost. At first I dug holes around the garden and dumped weeds, kitchen parings, and leaves into them to bump up the quality of the soil. All free. I didn't even bother to dig in the well-rotted compost. This approach worked so well that it has become a habit. Place the compost around the garden, and the worms will do the work for you. This is called top dressing.

Eventually, I had a composter made of leftover bits of wood. It was free and the compost, of course, is free. As far as I can tell, with thirty-odd years of gardening experience under my belt and never having once used a commercial chemical fertilizer or herbicide, you don't need them to have a healthy garden. So being an ecological gardener is a money-saving habit.

Buying compost and mulch is expensive. Making your own costs nothing but a tiny bit of effort and very little space. The optimum size for a compost bin is 4 feet by 4 feet, but you can make a composter in any small space. Here are a few more tips:

1. Layer green (grass clippings, kitchen waste, weeds) with brown (manure, soil, blood meal).
2. Turn the compost once a week or after every big dump of kitchen waste, and you'll be astounded at how fast this

mixture heats up and how quickly you have some compost to distribute.

3. Mulch by using a combination of ground-up leaves, compost, and composted bark. Spread it around the garden in autumn when the temperature is cold enough to create a hard frost. Scrape it off in spring, and toss it into the compost pile. This process will allow the soil to warm up quickly.

4. Mulch again once warm weather arrives (and you can start seeing weeds sticking their noses out of the ground). Chances are, you will not have to weed.

Gardener Diane McClymont-Peace says she uses a mix of mulch and newspaper topped with compost to retain moisture in her garden. She has installed a pond that stores rainwater, and uses the rainwater for her garden.

"Improvise," advises gardener Marilyn Weibe. "A length of the wire structure used to strengthen concrete flooring can be fashioned into a circle and used for a composter for yard waste and leaves."

Watering

The frugal gardener would never do a foolish thing such as watering the lawn at noon. Instead, we use barrels filled with rainwater to water plants, especially since it's chlorine free. Here are some other water-saving tips from our thrifty gardeners:

- Welcome used equipment from others, such as wheelbarrows and rain barrels, to gather rainwater for the garden. But don't let mosquitoes breed — use up the water quickly.
- Install a rain butt (a rain barrel attached to the runoff from the eaves). It should have a spigot insert at the height where you can remove water easily into a watering can. If you don't, you'll forget you have water in there festering away. Always empty the rain butt at the end of the season.
- Attach a pliable plastic cuff to the end of your eaves, and aim it at the garden. A lot of water comes off the roof, off your eaves, and this reuse keeps a lot of water out of storm drains.
- Water very early in the morning or in the early evening. Never water at midday when most of the water evaporates.
- Water stressed-out droopy-looking plants by hand. A few buckets of water in the right place will fix up most plants.

Watering systems are very expensive. Unless you find an exceptional company, they will probably be installed by someone who has never gardened. They are programmed to run every fifteen minutes, several times a week, which creates a huge amount of waste. Either get a good hose with a brass nozzle and water the garden yourself, or make sure the system you use can be turned on manually. The water should be capable of percolating through the soil to below the root systems of trees and shrubs, if it's to do any good at all. A slow dribble all around plants is the most economical way to go at it.

If you must have a watering system, use a drip system that you can turn on and off yourself. One of the most miserable wasteful sights: a watering system that runs during a rainstorm.

Weeds and Other Garden Pests

I try to attend to my garden every day in one way or another. Some days are devoted to pulling out those irritating violets. Another day it's lily-of-the-valley removal. And I always leave a stand or two of goldenrod (bumblebees and other good insects need them).

I'm a puller of weeds rather than a tiller of soil. I don't even own a good old Dutch hoe anymore because it was getting so little use. I try not to disturb the soil. This changes the soil structure and disturbs the microorganisms below. A heavy mulch keeps the garden pretty clean.

Our thrifty gardeners were not overly meticulous when it came to dealing with weeds. Diane McClymont-Peace has a schedule for weeding. She rotates a few beds every day. This practice prevents weeds from taking hold and causing any need for extensive weed control. However, she says, "The more I use newspapers as much of the composted mulch, the less I worry about weeds. I hand-weed before the plants go to seed, and take daily or biweekly walks through the garden to check on pests. I still use soap and water and other homemade remedies for reducing pests."

In April she starts "to save eggshells and crush them to use around hostas, which prevents slugs from climbing up the young leaves and devouring them." Here are some more tips on how to get rid of those pesky garden pests:

- Make your own insecticidal soap using 1 teaspoon of bleach and 2 drops of dish soap to 40 ounces of water. Place the liquid in a spray bottle. Use this homemade insecticide on any plants that are subject to aphids, especially roses.
- Pull out dandelions by hand. Chase the rabbits, reduce the number of lilies (because of the lily beetle), and ignore earwigs. Essentially, go with the flow.
- Use natural fertilizers and corn gluten for weed control.
- Spray spring flowers with a mixture of egg and garlic made in advance. It helps keep deer away.
- Get a box of Irish Spring soap, cut it in half, and insert each portion into some old pantyhose. Place each piece of soap strategically around the garden. Deer seem to hate it.
- A combination of vinegar and salt, 8 parts to 1, plus 1 teaspoon of dish detergent makes for a great weed killer. Be

very careful where you use it because it will kill *everything*. But it works well if you've got really nasty weeds between pavers.

- Pour boiling hot water over weeds, especially the ones working their way through stonework.
- If Coke can clean rust off an engine, don't be surprised at what it will do to weeds.

Bugs bug as well, though I'm not bothered by a lot of them. The following formula for white birch, pine, and ash is from gardener Henry Dobson: "We put a box of borax into a large pail of water and let it soak for a couple of days. Stir two or three times a day. Borax does not dissolve into a solution, but makes for a strong water mix. When you are ready to spray, draw a pillowcase tightly around the opening of the sprayer, and pour the contents into 30 to 40 gallons (115 to 150 litres) of water. Leave the pillowcase with residual borax hanging tightly to the opening. The contents of the pillowcase will then avoid plugging up the spray nozzle — this is important. Soak all sides of the trunk — we use an estate sprayer. The spray will penetrate to the heartwood of the tree. The time to spray is between April 15 and May 15. Trees that are well sprayed (from the ground up, to 8 to 10 feet) are deadly to insects located in the bark and will kill any beetles in the interior chomping on the wood."

Gardener Diane McClymont-Peace uses neem oil spray on the

ground around her lilies to prevent the almost unkillable lily beetle from emerging. She buys neem oil in bulk at Indian-food wholesalers or flower shows.

Juliet Mannock says, "Stop fussing and ignore weeds." She actually leaves only dandelions because "their deep roots provide passages for earthworms. Their leaves are also delicious in salads, or steamed — similar to spinach."

I can't ignore weeds altogether because I like mucking about my garden, feeling useful. Weeding is one of those Zen activities you can do alone, and it makes you feel like you are doing well by doing good.

SHARING A GARDEN

Gardening friends have always been the best people to turn to for any information or advice I've needed to garden successfully. I have friends I go shopping with, and I believe profoundly in creative stealing: if they've got good ideas, I don't mind lifting them straight from their shopping baskets into my garden. I have one friend with whom I shop so often that sometimes I just buy what she buys because her taste is superb. We share our gardens, our plants, and our ideas. With gardening friends you are always learning.

And swapping plants, of course, is on old and honoured gardening tradition, but there is a protocol to follow:

🌳 Never say: "When you want to get rid of that plant, I'll take some." Gardeners never want to get rid of plants. If you admire a plant enough, you'll be asked: "When I decide to divide this plant, would you like a piece?" Be sure to have something that's just as choice to offer in exchange or offer to buy the plant. Makes us feel good.

🌳 Always keep a piece of an incredible plant for yourself. I was given a piece of *Uvularia grandiflora* decades ago. Who knew then that it was one of the great native beauties of the eastern forest's spring garden? Well, I shared it all right and it finally ran out. I had to go out and buy more. Always keep a good chunk of a plant for yourself in more than one spot.

🌳 Volunteer to help out at plant sales, and you'll get a good crack at the best.

Barry Parker is a hortbuddy with whom I exchange plants and who is very generous with the many plants he grows. He is a huge believer in the don't-ask-for rule. He's also a keen observer of the garden: "Look around when you are weeding, you can often find seedlings from interesting plants, such as *Pulmonaria* and *Heurcheras*. They may end up being unique to your garden."

This business of being mindful of where you are and what you are doing is an essential element of gardening. Spend time peering under and around plants. Look into the faces of blooms to see their strange magic and mystery. Don't be terrified of bees. If you don't swat at them, they will leave you alone. Our survival depends on them.

Horticultural Societies

Just about everyone we canvassed through my web site and the national garden network urged the same thing: join a local horticultural society or botanical garden. These organizations usually have good speakers, garden tours, gardening information, and will tell you where the best nurseries and gardens are. You'll learn tips about which plants grow well in your area. Most of them have plant sales, and seed and bulb swaps. A hort society with a niche (rock garden, geranium, bonsai) may have extraordinary treasures for low prices, plus the rich knowledge of the people who are selling them.

Don't be a snob because you think these outfits are run by a bunch of old dears. A lot has changed in the past twenty years in the gardening demographic. Once people own a house or condo, they start gardening. They may put it on hold during financially difficult times, but a balcony and a pot of plants can turn any barren place into a home. Besides swapping plants, hortsocieties are great "meet" markets. You'll never suffer from boredom or be without friends if you get in with a bunch of gardeners.

THE GARDEN GODDESS

Uli Haverman is one of the true garden goddesses: she works in a nursery, has a gorgeous garden, and is also an intrepid plant collector. What Uli has to say is the perfect summing-up of the frugal gardener:

- It is important for people to get in touch with their own desires and have a hand in creating their own garden spaces. A person's garden should contain a collection of their favourite plants suited to that location.
- Do your homework. Talk to people about their successes and failures. Research and read everything you can about plants and possible design possibilities.
- Buy the best plants that you can afford. Even if you can buy only one plant per year, better to get a great plant than settle for something mediocre.
- Pay attention to soil amending. Make your own compost and save all those leaves that your neighbours rake to the curb. Chop them up with the mower and spread when the ground freezes. You will have the most beautiful ground cover for those long winter months.
- Stretch your budget by placing shrubs, trees, and perennials in planters and over-wintering them in the ground or in an unheated garage to reuse these plants again and again.
- Water once or twice a week but for several hours at each location. Plant succulents in containers when watering is an issue.
- Lawns play an important role in the design of a garden in that, like art, they act as a negative space to the positive space that is the garden. If you didn't have a lawn,

it would have to be replaced with some other medium that functions the same way, like paving. Lawns, however, allow for water percolation, earthworm activity, and an open space for chopping up leaves with the lawn mower.

- Keep weeds under control by planting thickly and deal with pests by hand. Or just get rid of the plant that attracts the pests.
- If a plant is too high maintenance, replace it with one that isn't.
- If time is an issue, start working on the garden the minute the snow melts and do a little bit every day. Complete small jobs before going to work in the morning and when you're back home at night.
- Be methodical and patient. Work in stages: amend the soil before planting; don't feel compelled to fill empty spaces; wait until you fall in love with something before you decide on what to plant next.

Like Uli, most frugal gardeners are always looking for the next great plant, fantastic container, or lovely piece of garden art, and they are saving up for the day when it finds them.

Organizing a Plant Sale

Karen York told me she once saw a big plant sale sign by the highway near Victoria, British Columbia. She turned to her husband and said, "Let's go look at the pots of goutweed and Cerastium." To her surprise, she actually found some good plants — well grown, well potted, and well labelled. She got three good clumps of black mondo grass and two "Key Lime Pie" *Heucheras* for a total of $10.

Now, that's certainly a bargain, but Karen's experience is a rare event. Plant sales are double-edged swords. People usually share the stuff that grows much too vigorously, so you end up with pots and pots of lily-of-the-valley, sedge, and creeping Jenny. Keep all of them out of your garden if you can.

But there are great reasons to have a plant sale: it gives you an excuse to divide plants, which has to be done every few years anyway, and it allows the garden to pay for itself. If you have enough friends to put on a plant sale, be organized. Here are a few hard-earned tips:

- Start digging up and potting plants a month before the sale.
- Wash out pots before putting in new plants. These vessels can sustain diseases for a long time.
- Use a good potting-soil mix and make sure the plants are robust and watered regularly. A well-grown plant fetches a high price.
- Use different-sized pots to represent different price points. Or get a bundle of Popsicle sticks from the dollar store, record the prices on them, and stick them in the soil.
- Label the plants and identify them accurately (botanical and common name). If you have space, list the plant's sun and shade requirements and whether or not they are drought tolerant.

It is also important to make sure you have enough people to handle the crowd, one person to handle nothing but the money, and another couple of people to handle the questions. You'll find that the customers who show up may be visiting a plant sale for the first time. They are looking for bargains and for knowledge. Be ready.

Be sure to have plenty of water, food, and wine for post-sale activity such as counting money. It's astounding how much you can make on a sale, but you'll be earning every single penny. So figure out if the money earned divided by the time spent is really worth it. We made $2,000 on the last plant sale we had, but it took three of us a month of work and when we divided our earnings, we weren't paying ourselves much an hour. But the event was fun, which made it worthwhile.

The Alternative Sale

If you can't stand the huge amount of organization a plant sale takes, send a list out to your friends and eager buyers describing what you've got and what they sell for. Then let them come and pick up the plants on a specific day. Have their orders organized and be prepared: they'll want other plants as well.

Gardening is not a short-range project. Think in the long term. Amortize what you spend in the garden over several years, then consider the value it's adding to your house (up to 10 percent). You'll see being active in the garden makes good fiscal as well as spiritual sense. But no one can really put a dollar value on a garden.

Gardening should be fun, not overfilled with rules. It can, however, be daunting if you go at it too quickly or without a little bit of help. Wander about nurseries, and you will see some of the happiest and most frustrated people on earth: the ones who are grateful that they can work with plants and the ones who don't know what they are doing. The thrifty gardener will stand back, figure it all out, and then dive in long and deep.

CHAPTER 6

THE THRIFTY
TRAVELLER

To the thrifty of mind and soul, travel seems to be at the top of the Must Have, Must Do list. When we were children, our family travelled all across North America staying in tents, camps, and in the car. We loved these trips, but I have lived long enough to know that it's a whole lot more fun travelling in comfort. How my parents stood three squabbling children and an uncomfortable night's sleep is beyond me. But it was fun for us kids because our memories are filled with images and experiences from these monumental trips. They are permanently etched into my brain, and that's one of the key tips about thrifty travel: it's about the experience you create, not how much you spend to create the experience.

GETTING THERE

Almost everyone I know books flights through the Internet. As freelance journalist Domini Clark advises: "Research, research, research. I actually determine a lot of my trips simply by where it's cheap to fly. I always have my eyes out for seat sales. Ryanair and Easyjet, for example, are fantastic ways of getting around Europe for cheap. Expedia, SideStep, Hotwire, and many other web sites are great for getting deals on flights." Students can also get special deals through travelcuts.com, and youth passes are available for bus and rail.

Domini has personal rules for thrifty travel, starting with: "Never trust a travel agent." I, on the other hand, have had good luck with travel agents. Every single dollar I have is important, and I want the kind of assurance a travel agency guarantees.

If you book flights through your local airline, make sure to get a direct flight. Expedia and other web sites offer cheap flights, but they often involve switching planes or layovers — and the cost of your ticket does not cover overnight accommodations. But if a direct flight isn't at the top of your priority list, then you can save money taking the scenic route to your destination.

ACCOMMODATIONS

Where you lay your head to rest can ruin a trip or make it your best experience ever. There are many ways to find relatively inexpensive places to stay, but most require some effort.

Swapping Your Home

Many travellers choose to look online for people in other parts of the world who are willing to swap apartments to save on accommodations. The trick is to find someone in the part of the world you want to visit who plans on travelling to your city or town on the same days. Make sure you don't leave anything behind you don't want stolen or damaged. I have heard of swaps that have worked out beautifully and others that have turned into a nightmare, so forewarned is forearmed.

Another form of swapping is to trade houses with a willing participant. In almost all cases you have to become a member of a service provider, and you must be away for longer than a few weeks. You've got to leave your accommodations in immaculate condition, and you pray that your home will be in good shape when you return. The savings are enormous. Find other people who've tried it and listen carefully to their stories. We heard about one Toronto couple who swapped with people in London, England. Instead of taking their swap at the same time, the Torontonians went to their cottage. When it came time to pick up their end of the swap, the London couple had sold their lovely flat. *Caveat emptor*.

Renting an Apartment

Since we started travelling together, Jack and I have learned that we are nesters. We like to go away, rent a place (usually a cramped little space

COUCHSURFING

Twenty-one-year-old Andrew Matlock discovered www.couchsurfing.com as a Canadian student living in England. He gave it a try with his friend Kim when they decided to visit Paris. Here is his story:

Couchsurfing.com is a free community service that allows one to either host or stay with complete strangers anywhere in the world. It may sound dangerous, but there's a sense of security with all the personal references and the ability to customize exactly whom you want to stay with. After some careful profile editing and searching (it's the equivalent of operating Facebook), we soon had a match with Jérôme. He lives just outside Paris and seemed very friendly.

Once in Paris, he very kindly picked us up (after we'd first gotten lost — make sure to get a phone number) and took us to his home. Jérôme owned the apartment building, which he was renovating. He lived in a beautiful top-floor flat, and when we arrived he made us an authentic gourmet French meal. Then he showed us where we'd be sleeping — an unrented apartment right next to his. Guaranteed, we were the luckiest tourists in Paris that holiday! I don't imagine all surfers would get coordinated pick-ups, food, or their own penthouse, so it was a bit of beginner's luck.

On the flip side, Kim and I had to share a bed (no problem for us, but make sure you're comfortable with any travel buddies), the only top-floor access was a five-storey spiral staircase, and Jérôme had a cat that wandered our floor. Now, I'm horribly allergic to cats, and it was a hairy thing. Sleeping in its proximity gave me a terrible flu and cough, burned my eyes, and left me wheezing up the Eiffel Tower the next day. But hey, we could also see the glittering tower from our own front windows.

with a great view), and make it our own. This ruins you for staying in hotels because renting is so much cheaper. You can eat in, save money, and live the life of the locals.

Over the years we've learned a lot about renting apartments in a foreign land. It's always best to visit the location first (as a tourist), and when you fall in love with it and are sure to visit again, then scout a good agent for the *next* trip. The first time you visit a new city, you often want to go everywhere and see everything. When you decide you want to return, you're less interested in the tourist sites and more interested in living and enjoying that culture's way of life. Build a relationship with agents by interviewing them and looking at the places they recommend. You can enjoy great savings: they do all the work finding you a place in your price range, and will make sure everything functions.

Rental apartments tend to be very small since most areas of the world don't have the luxury of space we enjoy in North America. So read those ads with a heavy dose of salt. A vast apartment can translate to a kitchen, living room, and bedroom in what feels like the space of a large closet. *Petite vue de mer* means if you stick your head out the window, with field glasses you'll be able to see the water. It doesn't matter; the apartment is a place to sleep and rest. When you're travelling, you'll want to spend most of your day out and about, discovering your splendid surroundings. Here are some tips on renting an apartment abroad:

- All rentals insist on a lease and a security deposit, which seems like an enormous amount of money up front. It will be returned to you. You hope.

- Some owners use the security deposit as a way of fixing up the place you've just rented — after you've left.

- Catalogue the condition of the apartment as soon as you arrive. Document any damage: malfunctioning light switches, fridges, and stoves; scuff marks on walls and doors; as well as missing bits from the kitchen. Take the list to the agent or owner and say, "This is the condition we found the apartment in, and we will not be paying for repairs or replacement of any of the following." In Europe they will respect you for your canniness.

We've never regretted renting either from an agent or directly from the owner. You are getting something comfortable enough, but remember these rentals are like cottages or cabins. They're usually furnished with leftovers and filled with mismatched pots, pans, and plates. But none of that matters. You are living in the skin of a real resident, and not just visiting like a tourist.

On Freeloading

Broadcaster Jill Dempsey says that if anyone invites her to come and stay with them in another country, she'll more than likely take them up on the offer. "It's a huge money saver," she admits. She has a self-imposed set of rules for this very frugal way of travelling. When she arrives, she asks her host, "How is this going to work? What can I do for *you*?" Here are Jill's other recommendations:

1. Make sure the hosts have a choice of turning you down. Make it easy for them. Always ask: "Are you sure this will work for you? You can say no, and you won't hurt my feelings."

2. Buy meals for your hosts when possible, or pick up groceries. If your hosts work, offer to make dinner and have it ready when they get home. Always remember that though you may be on holiday your hosts aren't; they will need to go to bed earlier than you do.

3. Look at their home strictly as a place to stay. Do not expect your hosts to be tour guides.

4. Offer to rent a car, but if you are loaned a car, leave it with a full tank of gas.

5. Strip the bed when you go.

6. Look around and see if there's something your hosts don't have that you can provide for them.

7. Always welcomed by worn-out hosts: a gift certificate for a spa.

Also check out couchsurfing.com's recommendations on how to be a good guest. It's terrific.

MOST COLOURFUL ACCOMMODATIONS   By Author Sylvia Fraser

Though I try to arrive at unknown destinations in daylight, an overnight train plus a twelve-hour bus ride landed me in Srinagar, Kashmir, in pitch-dark. The only passenger left, I was deposited under the boarded-up town's single light. About thirty men mobbed me, yelling, "Houseboat!" I accepted the one who yelled, "Taxi and houseboat," a man whose name I later learned was Abdul. The long dark drive, during which I became increasingly nervous, ended at a houseboat anchored at shore. My tiny room had only a curtain. Shadowy figures surrounded me from a second houseboat moored alongside. I was grateful to learn one was Abdul's wife.

Sunlight confirmed what I already knew — this spongy, listing houseboat was not one of the carved palaces featured in movies about the Raj. Though I intended to move out, I became fascinated by the family dynamic. Grandpa was obsessed with selling me a carpet and getting me to admit that the pine forests in the Canadian calendar I showed him had monkeys. Abdul made his hopes for me clear with photos of his last guest, whom he called his "English girlfriend." His teenage son kept delivering towels to my room when he thought I was undressing. Each morning Abdul's mother kneeled at my feet, clutching my velour slacks and telling me she had prayed all night to Allah that I would give them to her. Abdul's wife said nothing until the final day when, as I was leaving, she pulled off her sweater and began unfastening her bra. "A gift! A gift!" she said. I fled.

TRAVEL AND FINANCES

Dealing with exchange rates can be a pain in the neck. Always try to think in local money. If you are constantly translating you'll drive yourself crazy.

I habitually overpaid my Visa and then withdrew money from it when travelling abroad because the exchange rate was so good. But I stopped this practice when I managed to miscue my PIN number and the ATM ate my card. It took many long-distance calls, hundreds of dollars, and days of waiting to get a replacement card.

After that experience, I now use my bank card. I never forget the PIN number because I use it all the time. But make sure you find out what the bank charges for overseas transactions. They make money on both the exchange rate and the transaction cost. Withdraw as much money as possible each time so you won't be paying these charges as often.

Another tip is to open an account based on an area of the world you travel to frequently. I opened a U.S. account in Canada, and deposit some money into it every month. I pay exchange at varying rates, sometimes better than others. I found it a really good way to save up for a trip, and it's a habit I picked up from my friend Lynda who travels to London regularly. She buys pounds when she's feeling a little flush and puts them aside.

I also bought U.S. traveller's cheques for no charge with this account, and in the little town we stayed in the local bank cashed the cheques without charging a fee.

Sylvia Fraser is one of the most adventurous and thrifty travellers I know, and she's generously provided her main money tips:

- Divide up your spending money by the number of days away. Based on daily expenditures, this per diem will go up or down.
- Never take a taxi unless you're lost, it's late at night, or you're exhausted. A fact of travel: saving time usually costs money. Use local transportation, not just for economy, but for the adventure of getting to know a place. I've travelled by dogsled, donkey, camel, rickshaw (foot, pedal, and motor), every kind of motorbike with attachments, khlong, dugout canoe, sailboat, ferry, houseboat, train, and by buses piled high with livestock.
- As soon as I arrive at a new destination — before, if possible — I find out the going rate for various services. This is especially useful in countries where haggling is the norm. You do no one a favour — neither locals nor other tourists — by being a sucker or a lavish spender. Theft and corruption are often concentrated around major attractions because of tourist ignorance, gullibility, and misplaced charity. The *Lonely Planet* guides are an excellent source of local prices and circumstances. *Lonely Planet India* is probably the world's most stolen guidebook — not by locals but by other travellers.
- Flip side of the coin: don't play poor in a poor country. Don't try to get something for nothing. While you are working your

agenda, you're likely to miss that someone with much greater skill is working a nastier agenda on you.

Even if you travel at the level for which you've saved, whether frugal or fancy, build in one odd, unnecessary experience, such as getting a manicure. You'll find out amazing things by sitting there quietly for an hour. Bring a notebook so you can keep track of all your expenses. I love Moleskins and carry them everywhere, marking down shopping lists and what I've spent every day. For me it's fun, and it's a great record for the future, almost like keeping a journal. And I wouldn't consider travelling without a journal: how will you remember what you ate at every meal, what you saw, and how you felt in those exact moments? Travel is, above all, about enriching our life experiences by opening ourselves up to the world around us.

LE PACKING

Now that the airlines are limiting the amount of luggage you can take with you for free, packing light is a necessity. Take it seriously and you won't end up paying huge overweight-baggage charges. Here are a few rules on packing for a trip:

- Rule #1: Carry small bags. Large bags are difficult to manoeuvre.
- Rule #2: Invest in a well-made suitcase with wheels. A good one will last for years.

THE ARTIST'S WAY

"In India," says artist Prashant Miranda, "you can spend like a maharajah or a peasant. It's a culture that's thousands of years deep. Magnificent landscapes — deserts, jungles, tea fields, mountains, beaches, temples, ashrams." Prashant goes back to India for six months at a time. He travels with his watercolours, a backpack, and a small carry-on, and creates glorious sketches in his notebooks as he goes along.

"It just so happens," Prashant says, "that in my life, I work well with exchanges. So travelling with my art is the way I travel. People have invited me to stay in magical spaces/ resorts/hotels/homes, in exchange for a few watercolours or paintings or pieces of my art. I genuinely believe that it is in giving that we receive. On the other hand, I am lucky to say that I am blessed with many wonderful, benevolent souls who have kindly taken care of me. And I'm so grateful for that. I also love to cook, and if there is a kitchen available to me, I cook there. Very often I'm cooking meals for a bunch of friends in different spaces and in different cities. It's a great way to meet, catch up, and participate."

But what was Prashant's most memorable trip? "I took a train up to Moosonee once, and camped out alone on an island on the Moose River for a week. On the fourth day I saw the northern lights, which was an intense and very special experience. I have realized that the simple things in life are the most beautiful, and really don't have to be exorbitantly priced to achieve or experience."

- Rule #3: Only take what you can carry yourself, and can lift and store in the overhead bins.
- Rule #4: Make a list of what you pack and then tick off what you will actually use (keep a copy in your suitcase as well as on your person). This advice sounds obvious, but you'd be surprised at how often people don't do this prep work. It will become your basic packing list for all trips and a reliable document in case your luggage is lost.
- Rule #5: List your credit card, bank card, and passport numbers, and keep this information together.
- Rule #6: Don't confuse business with pleasure. For years I took an Issey Miyake suit (yup, I really went all out with this purchase because it was the perfect outfit to wear for giving speeches) with me on my travels because it rolls up into almost nothing. But I never wore the suit because when we travel, we dress casually. After three trips I finally realized that I was never going to wear this outfit and left it at home (with the exception of the pants, which were my all-time best investment).
- Rule #7: Never take clothing that needs to be ironed or dry cleaned. All of our thrifty travellers mentioned this point.

The following is my husband Jack's packing list for a one-month trip. All of the items fit into a small bag. I try really hard to follow his example, but I've added a few things that I throw in as well. We can go away for four to six weeks with three small bags plus a personal carry-on each. Even still, we have friends who find that this amount of luggage for a one-month trip is still way too much.

Jack's Packing List

For Wearing or Carrying on the Plane
Walking shoes
Socks and underwear
Jeans
T-shirt under a shirt
Sweater
Coat
Toque (Note: no scarf or gloves)

In Carry-on
Computer and plug
Two magazines
MP3 Player

In Hand
Book

In Suitcase
Four pairs of socks
Four pairs of underwear
Three button-up shirts
Two T-shirts
Two sweaters
Two pairs of pants
Sandals (to wear in apartment)
Rain jacket
Shaving kit: shaving cream, razor, toothpaste, toothbrush, dental floss,
sleeping pills, comb, shampoo, sunscreen
Vitamins
Medication (aspirin, ibuprofen)

I've experimented with the female version of the list, and all of the items fit into a carry-on bag. But I also take another bag to accommodate scarves, a pashmina for layering, a pair of good shoes, lots of colourful strappy T-shirts to wear under shirts, and additional underwear. Here are a few of my personal packing tips to add to Jack's list:

- Coordinate clothing colour. Black and beige make for a nice background for brightly coloured T-shirts and scarves.
- Always travel with a stain remover.

- Add a swimsuit, just in case.
- Take one small handbag big enough to hold money, passport, and one credit card.
- Pack an oversized bag that folds up into almost nothing, and, unfolded, is great for shopping.
- I have a special case that fits onto the carry-on that holds all my plane needs: music, notebooks, novel, makeup, eye mask, and earplugs, as well as all my pens and refills and travel journal.
- The carry-on holds the computer and as much clothing as possible.

I have a friend who swears she attended a tea at Buckingham Palace, two balls, and a dinner, and travelled only with a carry-on bag. This is like Platonic form for me: ideal but unattainable.

HOW TO PACK EVERYTHING YOU NEED FOR ONE MONTH ANYWHERE IN THE WORLD USING A CARRY-ON AND A KNAPSACK By Globetrotter Jane O'Hara

I won't check luggage. When I get off a plane in Frankfurt and have to catch the next flight out to Venice, I want my bags with me. So, the question is how to get everything you need — notice I said *need*, not *want* — into a carry-on. The trick is to sort out what the weather is going to be like at your destination. So, just before you start packing, always check the weather. If you have a range of 6° C (43° F) to 21° C (70° F) and rain in the forecast, you will have a good guideline for how to pack.

Start with rain gear, since rain can ruin a holiday if you are unprepared. First, pack a pair of good waterproof shoes that you can walk in for miles if you have to. Next, get a pair of black, quick-drying hiking pants. Find some that look like a regular pair of black pants — not the ones with the big baggy pockets hanging out and that unzip at the knee and double as shorts. People will spot you as a yellow-bellied tourist from miles away. If the quick-dry pants are decent enough, then you also have one evening outfit. Throw in a couple of linen scarves, a jaunty sweater, and a few different sets of earrings, and no one will notice you've been wearing this gear all day long.

Add a thin merino-wool black turtleneck — when it rains, it's usually chilly and you'll need it for warmth, especially in the morning. I also always take a short raincoat with a hood — eliminating a hat and an umbrella. Wear the raincoat and the rain shoes on the plane. Stuff the raincoat pockets with things you need — your iPod, lipstick, lip balm, money, etc., which will leave more space in your suitcase.

Quick-dry underwear and socks are also a must — and you need only two pairs of each. Then add a good pair of walking shoes and a pair of sandals if the weather will be warm (also good for walking around in your hotel room). Pack the shoes in your knapsack. They take up too much room in a suitcase. Also, pack a smaller, soft-sided purse that you can use while sightseeing.

Add pants, one white shirt, and one jacket (which can be worn on the plane) that go with the shoes and sandals. T-shirts take up no space and can double as a pajama top. Basically, everything you bring must go with everything else. I mix taupe and navy — very classy and a nice change from black.

If you run out of room while packing, just wear it. Layer up on the plane. T-shirt. Shirt. Sweater. Raincoat. There are no airline rules about wearing too much on board.

Jack and Jane may be inspiring, but I'd be lying if I claimed to follow either of their packing lists to the letter. But I do try to keep things to a minimum. The intrepid Sylvia Fraser says: "Before packing that wheeled bag you take to New York, ask yourself whether you're going to be getting on and off a lot of buses, boats, etc. The convenience of the wheels may be offset by much lifting and tugging. Same with heavily structured backpacks. Unless you're a serious trekker, take soft luggage you can squeeze under seats. Cardinal rule: pack only what you can carry. Two smaller bags are better than a large one."

Our experienced travellers make it a rule never to take too much, and advise the following:

- Rolling garments instead of folding them will save a ton of room in your suitcase.
- Most vacation spots are casual and civilized, so you can always rinse out a few undies. You probably won't be visiting with the queen.
- If you ever put something in the bag and think, "I *might* use this," take it out. You won't.
- Travel with a backpack. It's much easier for negotiating stairs/transit.
- Streamline your makeup-and-beauty routine. You can live without eye cream.
- Take no more than two pairs of shoes.

⊚ Take travel-sized containers of shampoo, conditioner, and toothpaste that are acceptable in carry-on luggage.

When I pack properly, people ask me for directions. I look like I belong in whatever country I find myself in. Layering is customary, but if you must wear a down vest because it's freezing, team it up with a turtleneck and fling a cape over it with the dash of a great scarf. You'll look great, and not touristy. Forget about shorts unless it's the national costume, and be careful of those bare arms for all sorts of reasons (custom, bugs, sun). And, like Jack, I finally worked out a rota for the clothes that makes sense when travelling.

LOCAL TRANSPORTATION

I am not normally a tour person. But I've gone on a few, and the best ones were run by Linda Thorne. They are based on visiting gardens, eating well, and staying in classy hotels. But when she's on her own, Linda is the essence of frugal travelling. She always goes off-season when she can get a good deal; she always stays in self-catering apartments rather than B&Bs or hotels. And, if she can, she will split the cost of accommodations with one or two others to slash her expenses dramatically.

In Europe she always checks to see if there are local passes for transportation and uses the city as a hub to take day trips by bus or to outlying areas. She much prefers this mode of travel to packing up and moving on. Travel is her personal luxury, and she is frugal in other areas of her life to be able to afford it.

Domini Clark says, "Don't take cabs to and from the airport." I don't mind spending money on a cab, limo, or shuttle bus to and from the airport, but this is highly personal. Domini also suggests embracing public transit, and I couldn't agree more. Some of the best experiences we've had on the road are on public transportation. Many parts of the world have great buses with inexpensive rates, and, in most cities, you can get day or weekly passes.

Some cities, such as Paris, offer shuttle buses that will take you right to your hotel. This turned into a wonderful experience for us one time: we came into the city in an early morning bathed in a pale golden-pink glow, and our driver described every major landmark as we drove by. Sadly, I didn't have a pile of euros to shower him with as a tip. I wouldn't do that next time. Always have with you at least $10 in local money for just such an occasion.

It always pays to check the fine print on the back of a ticket. The Paris Pass, for instance, is very expensive because it includes a lot of attractions that you may or may not want to do in a day or two. It's cheaper to buy ten tickets at the metro, and pick and choose where you want to go.

London, England, has its Oyster card, which allows you to hop on and off buses to your heart's content. It's actually fun getting lost, and the locals will help you if you are friendly. But don't overbuy: they divide the city up into regions, and if you choose too many you'll never use up the distance.

FOOD ON THE ROAD

I love eating on the road. I want everything that the people around me are eating, and of course the way to get their food is to go to the local markets. Every town has at least one, if not two, market days, and some are spectacular. In the little town we stayed in for many years in France, Saturday was the special *marché* day. There was the young guy with his portable wood-fired oven, making *socca* (a kind of ambrosial pancake made with chickpea flour); the baker with his huge loaves of bread; the butcher who makes incredible *saucisses*; the cheesemakers; and the olive farmers with their different kinds of oil. It makes me hungry just thinking about them.

The road was made for picnics. We used to carry wineglasses wherever we went, and a collapsible backpack to lug wine and *pan bagnat* (the wonderful niçoise salad on a bun), and hike out to a little tree on Cap Ferrat. We could gaze at the most expensive real estate in the world and have our own private bit of paradise at the same time.

We travel everywhere with a basic nesting kit: tablecloth, four napkins, a few candles, and a good wine opener. It can make a drab apartment cheery, improve a hotel room, or work well for a picnic. We always carry a roll of duct tape that never leaves my bag — there is nothing worse than a curtain that won't close or a bag with a hole in it.

We have learned obvious but necessary things when it comes to being a frugal foodie abroad:

- Eat the main meal at noon. There are usually good specials featured in most restaurants during lunch hour, and they often include a glass of wine (becoming rare). Prices tend to be a bit lower as well.
- Eating dinner out in any restaurant anywhere is going to be a major outing. Save it for special occasions.
- Takeout food in some parts of the world is so good it can outdo most restaurant food. I will buy a local specialty, which includes meat, and add a mass more vegetables. If you hold up thumb and forefinger to indicate you want a serving for two, you'll get enough to feed three, four with vegetables added.
- In any new town, we always spend a day or two hoovering our way through bakeries to find the best multigrain, whole-wheat unadulterated bread possible. It's never cheap, but you tend to eat every slice and it's filling.
- Do *not* ever go into pastry shops. They are so gorgeous, so tempting, so expensive. But if you must buy, get one wee tart and split it. I, happily, travel with a husband who hates dessert, which is why he is thin and I am not.
- Never sneer at the local plonk. It might be the best wine you've ever tasted. Wine expert Konrad Ejbich says: "Ask for

the wine that is produced as close to the region as possible. It will pair up perfectly with the food. In wine-producing areas, you see people go into wine stores with huge empty bottles and the wine is siphoned into them from barrels and for exceptionally low prices. Drink it."

- The Slow Food movement, which emphasizes eating local food in season, is the best thing that ever happened to frugal types. It's the cheapest and best way to eat on the road.

- If you go into a restaurant in a foreign country and the patrons are all speaking English, back away. The restaurant will likely be overpriced and mediocre at best.

- Go to places where you have a hard time making yourself understood. Eat whatever they serve up and then smile blissfully.

- Don't eat breakfast in a restaurant or hotel. Buy some fruit and yogurt at the local grocery store instead.

- Carry a meal kit: a Ziploc bag with fork, knife, wet-naps, a thin flexible cutting board, salt and pepper packets, and maybe some mustard and/or mayo. Also, a Swiss Army knife and corkscrew are mandatory.

- Ask the locals where they eat. (It helps to know a smattering of the language.)

- University cafeterias can provide decent, affordable meals.

- Pay for bottled water in areas where water quality is an issue.

My own way of finding a reasonable restaurant is to check out where the construction, farm, or office workers are eating. Unlike North America, lunch is sacred in many parts of the world and requires good food and drink for an all-in price. I've been known to follow guys through the back streets of Venice, pad behind them in the French countryside and along the byways of England. Chances are, where they eat the food will be good, and it will certainly be an adventure.

One time in France, we found ourselves famished after biking to a thirteenth-century village way off the beaten track. I watched a construction crew troop into a little bar. When we walked in and looked around, no one was there. Turns out they had all headed upstairs. So we did the same and found ourselves in a huge sunlit room filled with long tables set with bottles of wine. We grabbed the first empty spots we could, *bonjour*ed everyone, and poured ourselves a glass of wine just like everyone else.

The patron came around with a huge pot of soup and dished it out. We had what was served, and when everyone else left I asked for another glass of wine. The waiter grabbed an open bottle from another table and plunked it down on ours. The whole experience was glorious. We visited the bar regularly after that, and they set a table aside especially for us. We got to love the owners because they made us feel so at home and not *les étrangers*.

I also discovered the best homemade pasta in the south of France at a truck stop, which also happened to have a spectacular view of the whole Côte d'Azur — ten times better than the Michelin restaurants nearby. When I asked for a reservation (next to the window), they fell over laughing but made up a little card to please me. It was their very first request for one. The truck stop became a regular hangout for us, and when they closed we sent messages of condolence.

The point I'm trying to make is that this habit of habituating makes life so much easier for the thrifty traveller. Running around trying to hit all the tourist sites means you don't see much of anything or get a strong feeling for where you've been. Slow travel is the only way to go. Do less, learn more, savour everything. Never rush travel. It costs too much in both money and experience.

MORE THIFTY TIPS FOR TRIPS

When it comes to travelling, Karen von Hahn sums it up beautifully: "When I travel, I am extremely wealthy." Our fearless correspondents all had splurges and savings suggestions for the road. Here are their recommendations for where to splurge and where to save:

- Splurge: A good restaurant. A nice bottle of wine or some local specialty.
- Splurge: A side trip to a neighbouring town or city that sounds interesting.
- Splurge: Local shopping for quality items you might not find at home.

- Save: Check out local papers, flyers, and posters to see what kind of entertainment may be available either for free or for modest prices.
- Save: Markets and grocery stores are *the* places to buy affordable gifts and local specialties for people back home.

Though so many of our thrifty travellers said to forget about shopping, my motto is: if you see it and can't live without it, buy it. The coveted item probably won't be there the next time around, and it will always be more expensive *if* you can even find it back home. I don't buy much: olive oil from a small farm, *fleur de sel*, and maybe a few T-shirts. But I always have a budget ceiling in mind. I make deals with myself. If I can make a little extra money by writing a story, I can have this lovely item. If I can't figure out how to do it, I don't buy anything.

WHEN IN ROME . . .

The older I've gotten the less I travel with. I've given up on trying to out-chic the French or Italians. But you should blend in with the locals as much as you can. If you don't stand out as a *tourist*, you'll be treated well.

In most countries I've been to, people are wonderful. They say good day, nod, or smile; they give you a good-evening, and always proffer advice on food. That's if you are cheery yourself and try to speak their language even with a minimum of skill. The thrifty traveller is the observant traveller. How are people around you behaving? What are they wearing?

Approach people with an attitude of entitlement (I'm spending money, you better treat me well), and you'll probably be brushed aside. Patience is always a requisite when you're in someone else's country. A smile always saves time, and ultimately it could save money. Look at the locals as your best resource.

STAYCATION

Airline travel has become so stressful, we know more and more people who are saying phooey on it. And in tight money times, staying at home has become the new holiday norm. What you save on travel expenses can be applied to exploring a new part of your city or a nearby town. I have been tempted to check into a great little hotel, book a special dinner out, wander around my city, maybe have a little spa treatment, and go home refreshed. And most of us know we have some of the best tourist attractions in the world right around us.

Here are some tips on how to make the most of a vacation at home:

1. Look at your city through the eyes of a stranger and research all that it has to offer.
2. Check out weekend papers for hotel package deals. Some hotels even have one-night deals, which might include museum passes or other specials.
3. Buy a transport pass that will give you unlimited trips for a day or a week. Riding around on public transportation can be revealing, relaxing, and perhaps lead to an adventure. You can

hop off and try that restaurant you've never had time for way on the other side of town.

4. Dinner-and-theatre packages are always on offer and are not hugely expensive.

5. Museums and libraries host speakers, music programs, and plays for children.

6. Parks departments often offer eclectic activities, such as square dancing and even clown school (only for children).

7. Most towns and cities have great summer theatre. Free theatre in the park is a specialty in many cities.

8. Volunteer at the local jazz, writers', theatre, or music festival, and you'll get a free ticket.

9. Visit a farm. I am a member of CSA (Community Supported Agriculture), and they organize trips to member farms, where you can put in a healthy day of weeding and then eat the bounty of the harvest. It makes for a day's outing for the whole family, and it doesn't cost you anything. The kids might learn where their food came from, and you'll have enjoyed some great eating.

10. Consider getting out your bike or renting one; or buy a pair of good hiking boots and head for the countryside.

11. Most cities offer walking tours. Toronto, for instance, has Murmur tours: you rent a mobile phone, walk to different locations, and your phone guide will give you the history of the various sites.

12. Ferries and boat tours are a wonderful and relaxing way of taking in your city's sites.

The staycation is about being creative and enjoying what your hometown has to offer — a luxury in our increasingly busy lives.

Whether crossing an ocean or just crossing the street, thrifty travelling is about the experiences you create and the memories you keep. I adore travelling with my husband. We are good companions, we laugh a great deal, and after a thousand years of marriage our habits don't get on each other's nerves. We would never give up travelling because of money — old age or death will be the end of it, but not a minute before. The frugal traveller is the smart traveller, the one who spends little but gets a whole lot out of life's experiences.

CHAPTER 7

THE TOP 20 TIPS FOR LIVING THE FRUGAL LIFE WITH STYLE

My hope is that if we look at the thrifty life as an adventure in how to save and how to savour the minutiae of our daily lives, we will embrace the richly frugal life. In fact, thrifty living can be a lot of fun.

I learned an incredible amount talking to so many people who had creative ideas about money and living well. One of the major points they made was that to become a thrifty citizen you must examine your life carefully. From fashion to food to home, garden, and travel, frugal living is about rethinking our values and what we do with our time. I was particularly touched by Stevie Cameron's comment about cooking for the homeless: the idea that she and the other volunteers were being thrifty not just by cooking delicious food but by being thoughtful about what they served. It's a principle that can be applied to every aspect of our lives.

Tips on living the frugal life with style are found throughout this book. Here are the twenty that made the biggest difference to me. Though they are not in order of importance, they all have significance for the thrifty way of life

1. Understand the difference between your needs and your wants. Being thrifty means being self-aware.
2. Define and redefine your needs until you are confident that you know just who you are.
3. To thrive is all-important. Being thrifty should enhance a feeling of well-being rather than deprivation.
4. De-clutter your life. Organizing your life is the first step toward organizing your finances.
5. Always have a budget in the supermarket, in the garden, in life.
6. Never borrow more money than you can afford to pay back.
7. Consolidate your debts.
8. Figure out your net worth; you may not be as poor as you think.
9. Take a percentage of everything you make and save it monthly.
10. Become money literate.
11. Always do your research before making any purchases, big or small.

12. Read the fine print.

13. Buy well and you buy once. Quality is the hallmark of thrifty shopping.

14. Thrift is not about cost but about value and long-term emotional investment.

15. Avoid shopping as therapy.

16. Repurpose, repair, refit, reuse, resell, recycle: from food to fashion to home evolution, be creative and make the most of what you've got.

17. Never buy more than you need.

18. Don't throw good money after bad. Workmanship is at the heart of thrift.

19. Thrift is about the experiences you create, not how much you spend to create the experience.

20. The essence of frugality is quelling the desire for acquisition. It's about making things complete.

It came as a big surprise to some of my friends that I'm a thrifty person; maybe because I do live such a wonderful life and I'm very lucky. What seems on the outside to be a life of privilege is very carefully thought out. I have developed a good sense of what's important to me, in order to live a life of modest luxury.

When I was very young I started collecting art. I knew that I wanted to spend the rest of my life with these lovely objects. And I gave up other things to do so. I don't remember what I gave up because it wasn't nearly as important as having glorious paintings on the walls. I still plot on how I can save up for something of great beauty that will see me out. And I will always continue to live my life in a thrifty way — with style.

NOTES

INTRODUCTION: HOW I GOT TO BE THRIFTY
You can read more about me on my web site: www.marjorieharris.com

CHAPTER 1: THE THRIFTY CITIZEN
Atwood, Margaret. *Payback: Debt and the Shadow Side of Wealth.* Toronto: House of Anansi Press, 2008.

Clarkson, Adrienne. *Heart Matters.* Toronto: Penguin, 2007. A wonderful autobiography.

Lindsay, Janice. *All About Colour.* Toronto: McClelland & Stewart, 2008. One of the most useful books you'll ever read about colour and decorating.

Orman, Suze. *Suze Orman's 2009 Action Plan.* New York: Random House, 2008. A great guide to navigating your finances during precarious economic times

Check out www.truehelpfinancial.com, which is a great financial-organizing tool.

CHAPTER 2: THE FRUGAL FASHIONISTA

A web site that has lots of tips on thrifty shopping is http://www.wiki-how.com/Main-Page.

For more information on The Uniform Project, please visit www.theuniformproject.com.

Value Village has a great web site, www.valuevillage.com, which includes information on store locations, tips, and upcoming sales.

Olson, Sheree-Lee. *Sailor Girl*. Toronto: Porcupine's Quill, 2008.

Ashenburg, Katherine. *The Dirt on Clean: An Unsanitized History*. Toronto: Knopf, 2007. For more information on author Katherine Ashenburg, please visit www.ashenburg.com.

If the reader is interested in the works of Jack Batten, he has just published a new history book. Batten, Jack. *The War to End All Wars*. Toronto: Tundra Books, 2009.

CHAPTER 3: THE FRUGAL FOODIE

Do not miss www.greatcooks.ca. It's a superb web site and offers great recipes. Their olive oil is fantastic.

For more information on Ontario wines, take a look at this wonderful compendium: Ejbich, Konrad. *A Pocket Guide to Ontario Wines, Wineries, Vineyards, & Vines.* Toronto: McClelland & Stewart, 2005.

To follow Stevie Cameron and developments around her new book, *The Pickton File*, go to www.steviecameronblog.blogspot.com.

For the latest information on food and delicious recipes, visit Lucy Waverman's web site, www.lucywaverman.com.

CHAPTER 4: THE FRUGAL HOME

A great classified-ads site is www.kijiji.ca. It's easy to navigate and leads you to a wealth of web sites.

www.diynetwork.com has fairly articulate step-by-step shots of home renovations, and gives you an idea of how complicated things can get. Even if you don't take on a reno project yourself, it's always good to know what you are hiring other people to do.

For more information on Ted Johnston, please visit www.thelake-house.ca.

Freecycle.org is a terrific resource for finding free furnishings.

Visit www.cbc.ca to listen to Talin Vartanian's podcasts.

For more information on colour consultant and designer Janice Lindsay, please visit www.janicelindsay.com.

For more information on home decorators Lindsey and Gerry Anacleto, please visit www.anacletodesign.com.

You can find all of Edward O. Phillips's books for sale on Amazon.

Karen von Hahn is a regular contributor to the *Globe and Mail's* Style section. Check out www.theglobeandmail.com to read her columns.

For more information on HomeSense, please visit www.HomeSense.com.

CHAPTER 5: THE THRIFTY GARDENER

For more information on gardening and my gardening books, please visit www.marjorieharris.com.

Day, Sonia. *Middle-Aged Spread*. Toronto: Key Porter Books, 2009. A lovely memoir about moving to the country.

You can find great garden web sites through www.gardenwriters.ca. Mark Disero runs the site and covers garden events.

You can find a vast amount of garden information at www.torontobotanicalgarden.ca. Paul Zammit, who is Uli Haverman's husband, is as committed a plant person as she is and has made great contributions to this web site.

For more information on Eco-Lawn, please visit www.wildflowerfarm. com.

For great seed info, join ORG & HPS (Ontario Rock Garden & Handy Plant Society); see October 2009/10 Seedex, www.ontrockgarden.com.

CHAPTER 6: THE THRIFTY TRAVELLER

For more information on swapping houses, please visit www.homelink.ca.

If you're interested in couchsurfing for your next vacation, please visit www.couchsurfing.com. The web site also offers great etiquette tips for "freeloading" travellers.

Sylvia Fraser has a new book out called *Chasing the Cure* (co-authored by William Bengston), Toronto: Key Porter Books, 2009. Her travel book on India is not to be missed: Fraser, Sylvia. *The Rope in the Water: A Pilgrimage to India.* Toronto: Thomas Allen Publishers, 2002.

Take a look at artist Prashant Miranda's travel notebooks at www. prashart.blogspot.com.

For more information on local walking tours, please visit www.yourcity. ca to see what your area has on offer.

ACKNOWLEDGEMENTS

This book was Margaret Atwood's idea; Lynn Henry got the ball rolling and brought the wine for the discussion about how to do it fast. Janie Yoon was an unbelievable editor: great suggestions and organization, cheerleading par excellence, and she carried on with great humour against incredible deadlines.

Chris Harris created the questionnaires and worked valiantly on the research.

The following people sent in ideas, tips, and essays, and I fell madly in love with each and every one of them: Marla Allison, Lindsey and Gerry Anacleto, Jennifer Arnott, Katherine Ashenburg, Margaret Atwood, Jack Batten, Sarah Batten, Margot Belanger, Esther Benaim, Bev Brock, Judy Brunsek, Stevie Cameron, Mary-Ellen Campbell, Philippa Campsie, Derek Chu, Domini Clark, Anne Clark-Stewart, Adrienne Clarkson, Carol Cowan, Alix Davidson, Sonia Day, Sheila Delaney, Jill Dempsey, Mark Disero, Julie Dixon, Henry Dobson,

Monique Dobson, Konrad Ejbich, Moira Farr, Wendy Finnie, Sylvia Fraser, Deborah Fulsang, O.W. Gilmore, Esther Giroux, Miriam Goldberger, William Grainger, Bonnie Gray, Katherine Hajer, Jennifer Harris, Uli Haverman, John Howarth, Norma-Jane Howarth, Steve Huband, Lynda Hurst, Paul Jenkins, Ted Johnston, Cathy Jones, Deirdre Kelly, Nancy Kenyon, Elizabeth Kilbourn, Paul Lewis, Janice Lindsay, Susan Longmire, Hazel Luce, Juliet Mannock, Kelly Mansell, Laurie Matheson, Andrew Matlock, Stephen McClare, Lisa McCleery, Diane McClymont-Peace, Deborah McPhedran, Prashant Miranda, Karen Mondok, Valerie Murray, Gemma Norton-Wilkes, Jane O'Hara, Sheree-Lee Olson, Barry Parker, Edward O. Phillips, Kris Schultz, John Sebert, Patricia Shapiro, Gail Singer, Peter Smith, Sylvie Soth, Jim Stanford, R.H. Thompson, Linda Thorne, Beryl Tsang, Talin Vartanian, Daiene Vernille, Karen von Hahn, Judith Ward, Lucy Waverman, Marilyn Weibe, Marianne Wightman, Iris Wilde, Maggie Wrobel, Karen York, Colleen Zacharias, and Jane Zednik.

I apologize to those whose responses and stories didn't get quoted directly. Everything you told me did make it into my head and influenced the outcome of this book.

Finally, thanks to Koko Karunathan for her help and Jack Batten, who is my best friend and the world's most divine husband.

INDEX

ABOUT THE AUTHOR

Edward Pond

MARJORIE HARRIS has been called "a force of nature" and "a survivor with a will of iron and a heart of gold." At an early age, she learned how to live an independent life on very little. Born in Shaunovan, Saskatchewan, Harris lived in Winnipeg, Goose Bay, Labrador, Vancouver, Hamilton, and Toronto, where she eventually settled as a freelance writer and became the modern-living editor at *Maclean's*, covering food, fashion, and design. She is now considered the country's best-known gardener. She is the national gardening columnist for the *Globe and Mail*, and the author of several bestselling gardening books. She lives the rich but frugal life in Toronto, with her husband, writer Jack Batten.